APPRAISING TEACHING QUALITY

APPRAISING TEACHING QUALITY

John D. Wilson

HODDER AND STOUGHTON
LONDON SYDNEY AUCKLAND TORONTO

Changing Perspectives in Education

Series Editor: Noel Entwistle, BSc, PhD

The Core Curriculum Gordon Kirk
Improving Study Skills Ian Selmes
Understanding Classroom Learning Noel Entwistle
Appraising Teaching Quality John D. Wilson

British Library Cataloguing Publication Data

Wilson, John D. (John Dewar), 1939–
Appraising teaching quality —— (Changing perspectives in education).
1. Teachers. Assessment
I. Title II. Series
371.1′44

ISBN 0-340-40754-9

First published in Great Britain 1988

ISBN 0 340 40754 9

Phototypeset by Gecko Limited, Bicester, Oxon.
Printed and bound in Great Britain for Hodder and Stoughton Educational, a division of Hodder and Stoughton Limited, Mill Road, Dunton Green, Sevenoaks, Kent by Richard Clay Ltd, Bungay, Suffolk

Contents

The Series Editor

Noel Entwistle is Bell Professor of Education at Edinburgh University and Director of the Godfrey Thomson Unit for Educational Research. Previously he was Professor of Educational Research at Lancaster University and editor of the *British Journal of Educational Psychology*. His main research interests are in the field of student learning and motivation, and he currently chairs the Innovation, Research and Development Committee of the Scottish Micro-electronics in Education Committee.

The Author

John Wilson taught English in a comprehensive school in the sixties, and has worked in higher education since 1964. After lecturing in education at Aberdeen University, he was head of the department of education at Moray House College of Education, Edinburgh. His main research interests are the professional development of teachers, teacher assessment, evaluation and curriculum development. He is the author of *Student Learning in Higher Education* (1981).

Acknowledgments

I should like to thank the Scottish Education Department, especially Frank Bigwood and Bill Nicol, for supporting the project on selection for initial teacher training which enabled me to develop my thoughts about the meaning of quality in teachers and teaching. The Criteria for Teacher Selection (CATS) research team, and particularly its Research Associate, Lindsay Mitchell, shared with me the difficulties and the excitement of innovating with regard to teacher selection. Dr George Thomson gave valued support in his role as Chairman of the project's advisory committee. Noel Entwistle's encouragement for the writing of the present volume was much appreciated. I am greatly indebted to Helen Robertson and Ruth Simpson who so skilfully turned illegible manuscript into readable text.

The author and publishers would also like to thank the following for permission to reproduce material in this book: McGraw-Hill Book Company for the extract by B. S. Bloom from *Human Characteristics and School Learning* on pp. 22–3 and Figure 5.1 on p. 68; NFER/Nelson for the extract by J. Pearce from *Standards and the LEA* on pp. 32–3; Paul Chapman Publishing Limited for Figure 3.1 by A. McMahon from *Readings in School Based Curriculum Development* on p. 41; Bryan Dockrell for Figure 4.3 on p. 62; Academic Press for the extract by D. C. Berliner from *Research on Exemplary Schools* on pp. 73–4; Margot Cameron-Jones for the extract from *Focus on Teaching: Project Report* on pp. 83–4.

Introduction

The White Paper *Teaching Quality* (DES, 1983) described the teaching force as 'the major single determinant of the quality of education'. It not only put emphasis on improved selection and training of teachers, but also made the case for routine appraisal, a point taken up in *Better Schools* (DES, 1985). Government can now insist on appraisal and several pilot schemes are currently operating in England.

But if appraisal is to be linked to teacher quality, it is necessary to be clear about what quality means. Although much bandied about, it is rare to find any attempt to explain the term's practical significance, or the criteria on which the quality of a teacher's work is to be judged. This book attempts to do just that. It defines quality as the teacher's *capacity to deliver* (put into effect) *the optimum curriculum to the individual learner*. A central idea is consequently that of *matching* what is to be learned to individual needs. Delivery is *par excellence* the responsibility of the teacher, but what she is required to deliver is not necessarily of her own choosing. One of the perspective shifts which the book highlights relates to the importance attached to centralised planning through the creation of national curricular frameworks, and the equally important emphasis on school-based curriculum planning. Such planning may be restrictive or it can enhance the quality of a school's programme and support the autonomy of the classroom teacher. Certainly it is still the teacher who puts the curriculum into effect and the skill with which she arranges the learning process and matches tasks to pupils is a critical factor in the quality of pupil learning experiences. The proof of the teacher's effectiveness in the short-term lies in the work children produce, and evaluation which focuses on this kind of evidence – which is typically what Her Majesty's Inspectorate (HMI) look for in their inspections – can indicate the extent to which such curricular goals as balance and challenge in the work set are being achieved.

Today these goals are increasingly defined by the customers and clients of schools, such as parents and government, rather than by teachers themselves. *Better Schools* (DES, 1985) states unequivocally that 'education at school should promote enterprise and adaptability in order to increase young people's chances of finding employment or creating it for themselves and others'. The Parents' Charter has given parents more choice, and school government now gives external interests a bigger say in the way in which schools are managed. Falling rolls means that schools can be seen to be competing with each other for pupils. Such changes imply a responsive management in schools, with headteachers who are able to demonstrate professional leadership, and to prove that their school deserves to survive.

Recent studies of headteachers at work suggest that few have modified their approach to management in response to these new expectations. Some headteachers lack confidence in managing change, and practical suggestions are offered in several chapters on how they might improve the quality of their school programmes. However, some headteachers are simply not up to the job or are unable or unwilling to change.

Current procedures for the selection and training of headteachers have been widely criticised, as indeed have those for the selection of teachers for initial teacher training. Alternative models of selection reflecting operationalised criteria have been piloted, so that the means to improve formal assessment exists if the political will or the appropriate administrative structures to put them into practice could be found. Indeed, it is argued that it makes nonsense to introduce contentious systems of appraisal when assessment at the key points of entry to and promotion within the profession are so undeveloped.

Chapter 1 reviews some of the changing concepts which underlie the definition of quality today. These include the notion of what pupils should learn and what they are capable of learning, the meaning of planning and its relation to delivery, the need for innovation and how it should be managed. Chapter 2 examines how teaching quality has been defined at different times in the past, how it is defined today and how quality may be studied. In Chapter 3 the focus shifts to the school, to the expectations of clients and customers and to the ways they define the quality of a school, and how headteachers can bring expectations and reality closer. Chapter 4 examines the meaning of quality in planning at national and school level, and discusses how headteachers should manage planning, while Chapter 5 considers what quality of delivery by the teacher means and how the learning process can be effectively managed to establish and maintain a good learning environment in the classroom. Chapter 6 focuses on evaluation from the point of view of the results produced by pupils and the ways in which teachers can use self-evaluation to improve the effects of their teaching. Chapter 7 discusses appraisal in the context of formal assessment for teachers at the different career stages – selection for initial teacher training, appointment to teaching post, and granting of tenure and promotion. Reliable and valid assessment at these stages would put appraisal in its appropriate (minor) place as an aspect of staff development in a professionally managed service. The concluding discussion suggests that such a service could be created by establishing a national commission to manage the education service.

Sound empirical evidence is lacking for many of the issues discussed, and the conceptual framework needs developing. A policy for quality requires to be informed by research into the professional development of teachers.

In this volume, for the sake of consistency, the convention has been adopted of designating promoted teaching staff as 'he' and classroom teachers as 'she'. This is not to be taken to imply any endorsement on the part of the author of current sex bias in the distribution of posts in schools.

1

Changing Perspectives on Quality

I began teaching in 1961 after a two term 'crash' teacher training programme. I was rushed to a newly established comprehensive school near Glasgow to help fight the 'battle of the bulge'. The school had been formed by amalgamating a long-established grammar school with a junior secondary. Looking back I can see now that one of the (many) sources of tension in the school was competing definitions of quality. Some of the former grammar school staff spoke openly of the 'rubbish' they now had to work with – the pupils, that is! – and a sense of despair prevailed at the passing of an established order and the prostitution of their academic expertise. The merger was equally resented by some ex-junior secondary staff who had valued the freedom to teach what they liked to non-academic pupils. Some from both camps, however, shared the idealism of newcomers like myself who saw the comprehensive as the school of the future and had opted to serve there to promote its development.

This chapter attempts to provide a backcloth on changing perspectives on quality in education, and to simplify the presentation, I have set out ten questions worth asking. These questions are not the only ones that might be asked, nor are they necessarily the best. They simply provide pegs on which to hang a number of contrasts which are relevant to explore, as ways of thinking about the meaning of quality in education and the teacher's role in promoting it. The questions are addressed to those who manage the education service, but they could profitably be considered by people at all levels, from the most senior chief inspector to the rawest recruit to classroom teaching, since I believe that improvement of quality in education depends on people in the system as a whole coming to a clearer view of the criteria on which quality should be defined.

Ten questions about quality

1 What skills and qualities do you consider young people need to develop for the world they are about to enter?
2 What level of attainment do you consider pupils are capable of?
3 What importance do you attach to curriculum planning and how is this reflected in the way you go about it?
4 How do you see planning being reflected in the delivery of the curriculum?
5 How do you define quality of delivery?
6 How do you think a school's or a teacher's programme should be evaluated?
7 What institutional development policy have you formulated?
8 How do you manage the development of school staff and other personnel?
9 How do you manage and deploy resources
10 What are the most important policy issues you expect to be asked to tackle in the next few years?

There are likely to be many divergent answers to these questions, and these will reflect individual values and experiences, but there are certain trends which are clearly recognisable. In answering these questions the intention is to point up the criteria against which 'quality' will come to be judged in the future. The specific trends may change, but the analysis of what constitutes change should remain of value.

What skills and qualities do young people need?

At the turn of the century elementary and preparatory schools had a very clear conception of the skills and qualities to develop in pupils, and indeed of the role in society they would take up. Elementary schools were established to 'gentle the masses' to teach them to respect property (and authority), to learn that 'speech is silver, but silence is golden', and to assimilate the literacy skills that would enable the brightest to assume clerical roles, or climb the ladder to the new white collar posts in government and commerce. Preparatory (and public) schools went further to realise the official goal of an all-round education which balanced intellectual, moral, physical, spiritual and social development on the argument that 'the battle of Waterloo was won on the playing fields of Eton', and that breadth of vision was necessary for a class entrusted with the task of managing an empire. This was interpreted in terms of, initially, a classical curriculum with chapel, team games, Combined Cadet Force and an informal system of social moulding through prefects and fagging. External examinations dominated the curriculum of grammar and public schools. They rewarded written competence, knowledge of the syllabus and conformist attitudes. Within the school, respect for the authority of the teacher, the subject and its methods was inculcated: pupil initiative and freedom to challenge the assumptions and practice of the school were constrained. Progressive schools, such as A. S. Neill's Summerhill put a much stronger emphasis on pupil self-expression, but the immediate influence of such schools on mainstream practice was slight.

The emphasis on General Certificate of Secondary Education (GCSE) assessing what pupils 'know, understand and can do' reflects the contemporary perspective shift. The curriculum is the vehicle for the development of a range of skills – practical, social, personal – necessary for earning a living and responding creatively to the opportunities presented in modern society. A key idea is 'learning to learn' in a world of rapid and increasing technological and social change where the media are one universally accessible source of knowledge and ideas, and work-based learning is just beginning to be recognised as a valid source of certifiable competence which by-passes traditional routes to qualifications.

What attainments are pupils capable of?

Our assumptions determine our actions. In the past pupils were categorised as 'bright' or 'dull'. Subsequently there was talk of 'fast' and 'slow' learners. The founding fathers of pyschology assumed that mental attributes were 'normally' distributed like physical attributes, and constructed tests of verbal reasoning to demonstrate this.Teachers were trained to believe it. The assumption was institutionalised in the organisation of secondary education on tripartite lines, and in streaming within primary and selective secondary schools. Only the brightest were capable of entry to higher education, and even then the process of discriminating in terms of ability was reflected in the class of degree awarded.

Certainly there are differences in attainments of pupils. But how are they to be explained? The crude genetic explanation was modified by research in the fifties and sixties which pointed to the effects of social deprivation in early childhood, and resulted in massive intervention programmes such as Headstart. Sponsors were disappointed with the outcome, and the effectiveness of schooling itself was questioned. At the same time none could deny the evidence of wartime where school 'failures' had demonstrated the capacity to learn sophisticated skills, or of everyday life where similar success stories belied academic predictions. The perspective shifted to the appropriateness of the curriculum for the learner. Task analysis, developed to provide appropriate training sequences for pilots and tank drivers, and programmed learning pointed the way towards 'mastery learning', and towards structured learning experiences for the pupil. Today an optimistic philosophy is emerging which maintains that, in the future, the objectives of a programme should be capable of being attained by the vast majority of those who enter upon it. Success will be achieved through curriculum planning which leads to learning activities being structured in an optimum way for the individual student, and which uses a variety of resources to translate difficult skills and concepts into a manageable progression. In this new conception, key factors include allowing students sufficient time to learn and stimulating motivation.

What importance is attached to curriculum planning?

Every student teacher knows about the importance of lesson plans, but the classroom teacher was not under much pressure to produce them. Many local education authorities (LEAs) laid out the syllabus in schemes of work, and commercially-published language and maths packages were also adopted. Examination syllabi (and set books) obviated the need to do more than to decide how to work through content in the appropriate order.

At a time when the curriculum was static or slow changing, it was assumed that trained teachers knew what they had to teach. Local variation reflected teachers' attempts to provide for children's interests. Central government in the sixties took the view that the curriculum was the responsibility of LEAs and school staff. LEAs were reluctant to challenge the autonomy of headteachers, and in schools headteachers left planning to subject departments or to individual teachers.

The extent to which planning actually occurred depended upon the subject, the level of education, the attitude of the head of department and the conscientiousness and experience of the individual teacher as well as the standards prevailing in the school. At no time in three years can I recall a meeting of the English department being held in the school in which I served. I received memorable planning advice from my principal teacher on only one occasion, when I requested an additional set of class readers, having completed the first in half the expected time. 'Spin it out, John', he said, 'spin it out'. Part of the reluctance to plan stemmed from a feeling that it was obvious what to teach, as long as you kept a chapter ahead of the pupils, and part from a lack of certainty as to how to manage staff and how to go about planning. In *How Teachers Plan Their Courses*, Philip Taylor (1967) exposed these uncertainties and showed that secondary teachers' thinking was dominated by considerations of what would interest pupils, and by such constraints as accommodation and time rather than by design issues.

Individual teachers' practice varied, with some conscientiously preparing plans for up to a term ahead and developing sophisticated resources to support group teaching, while others viewed planning as impossible since flexibility, responsiveness and improvisation were essential for exploiting the potential of classroom encounters. Since heads of department, headteachers and advisers rarely asked for evidence of planning (although HMI might on school inspections) it often received only lip service, especially from teachers who taught by the textbook.

The change in perspective on curriculum planning reflects a number of developments of the sixties and seventies. First, there was the curriculum development movement following on from the establishment of the Schools Council in 1964. A new vocabulary for discussing curriculum design established itself. Behavioural and expressive objectives, mastery learning and issues in structuring and sequencing the curriculum to reflect modes of knowledge and realms of meaning surfaced as ways of talking about the curriculum, and it came to be realised that a wider range of choices was available to those responsible for planning. Many teachers involved in CSE mode 3 syllabus construction, or in curriculum development projects at national or local level, or through MEd or Open University courses became familiar with the terminology.

Second, the gap between the 'written' and 'taught' curriculum came to be recognised by evaluators who sought to explain different levels of implementation of the same project with different teachers. Surveys by HMI also pointed to a substantial gap between the official aims set for schools in national planning documents and the programmes actually experienced by pupils. Schools were criticised for failing to define clear objectives, and to ensure that what was provided reflected them. Teacher autonomy – sometimes interpreted as the right to ignore curricular areas, such as environmental studies, which the teacher felt ill-equiped to teach – was challenged, and the broad nature of the student's experience over the school day, week, term and year was investigated to see how far the programmes as a whole offered variety and challenge. Evidence of incompetence (William Tynedale) and muddle, together with an argument that national standards of achievement were not rising fast enough relative to the improved level of resources and training available, led to the Great Debate at the end of the seventies. (For an extended discussion of this issue see *Core Curriculum*, Kirk, 1986.) Emerging from this is the third factor. Government has now given itself and its agencies a more prominent role in relation to curriculum planning. It is providing clearer guidance to LEAs and schools on the framework of the curriculum, and is requiring schools to demonstrate how their programmes reflect the framework. Perhaps the most striking example of these new powers is the introduction of GCSE. The Secondary Examination Council published general criteria for the new certificate awarded for the first time in 1988 and specific criteria for the twenty most common subjects. As a condition of presenting students, schools are required to indicate how their courses match the criteria. In Scotland the development of Standard Grade (14–16) provided a blueprint for GCSE, while centralised control of all non-advanced further education courses has been allocated to a central agency, the Scottish Vocational

Education Council (SCOTVEC). In higher education the Council for National Academic Awards (CNAA) has enunciated principles of course design in its regulations. These principles have to be reflected in proposals submitted to it as a condition of validation.

Curriculum planning today is seen as a group as much as an individual activity. The group may be a subject department, an interdisciplinary team, or a headteacher and classroom teachers at a particular stage of the primary school. Outsiders may be involved. A plan must be consciously formulated, taking account of a range of interests and considerations; it must be 'owned' by all who have to put it into effect, and they must understand and be committed to it. Above all, it must be rational and defensible as a means of identifying and delivering appropriate curricular objectives with the emphasis on skills rather than subject knowledge. The new approach, then, attaches more significance to planning. The curriculum plan evolves from reflective discussion as to how objectives and criteria for a course can be realised through the envisaged learning experiences. This contrasts with typical former practice where planning was imposed autocratically or *laissez faire* prevailed.

How is planning reflected in delivery of the curriculum?

A teacher's actions in the classroom should reflect her planning. In the absence of planning, and with limited objectives, the teacher entered the classroom relatively unsupported. Teaching was an individual rather than corporate activity, conducted behind closed doors, with a limited range of resources, and with teacher-centred instruction predominating, pitched at the middle of the class. Class tests provided evidence of the mastery of the knowledge that was to be learned. Teacher–pupil relationships were formal, corporal punishment widely employed, backed up by 'sending out' of the classroom, exclusions from school and suspensions.

Curriculum planning has to be more sophisticated today because schools are expected to deliver a wider range of skills. Implementation of the plan is a corporate, as well as an individual, responsibility. Good planning should mean that an adequate range of resources exists to realise the plan. Teachers know what they are expected to do to put it into practice and employ a varied range of teaching methods, with the aim ultimately of individualising the curriculum. Tasks are selected consciously to match the capabilities of pupils. Assessment has been designed to provide evidence that pupils are making the desired progress to enable them to complete the course successfully. There is a rationale to the different parts of the programme which gives teachers confidence in what they are attempting. Morale among staff and pupils is high (despite the amount of work involved) because each feels supported and sees the relationship between the immediate and the long-term objectives. The quality of teacher–pupil relationships is good, since the basic relationship is a cooperative one, the teacher assisting the pupils to realise the objectives they wish to achieve. Of course, such an idealised view of planning is rarely achieved in curricula implemented today. Nevertheless the potential exists to make delivery a conscious process of selection of resources to achieve defined goals.

How do you define quality of delivery?

'Delivery', of course, is the 'in' word for face-to-face teaching in the classroom, but the word does emphasise the relationship between planning and teaching. In the past, the main emphasis was put on class control, knowing what you were teaching, and obtaining good examination results. Such elements are still important, but the definition of quality of delivery is broader today and includes the range of objectives being pursued, the balance between whole class, small group and individual work, the extent to which pupils with learning difficulties are identified and catered for, the range of resources employed and the skill with which their potential is exploited, and the human relations skills in coping with difficult and deviant pupils.

Publications such as *Teaching Quality* (DES, 1983) suggest that these skills are probably weakly developed in courses of teacher training even today. Primary school students are criticised for their lack of understanding of the principles of language and maths teaching, and their courses do not always give them confidence to teach aspects of the curriculum such as science and expressive arts where their own general education has been weak. Consequently, in the absence of school-level planning, teachers'programmes frequently reflect their own strengths and curricular interests rather than what would be balanced experience for their pupils. Recruits to secondary schools may also have a conception of their subject, out of tune with modern thinking in schools if their studies have been undertaken in a university department with little interest in the debate about the nature of the specialism.

Certainly with regard to core professional knowledge in aspects such as curriculum planning, progression, assessment and evaluation, teachers emerging from training programmes today are probably only slightly better equipped for the demands that will confront them than their predecessors of thirty years before. This reflects both the limited time available for initial teacher training, and also the static teacher training force, itself out of touch to some degree with recent developments in schools and in curricular theory.

How is the programme evaluated?

Schools traditionally pointed to such indices of academic performance as 11+ success or university entrance places, with pass rates at O and A level also being a matter of internal concern. Since certificate results were not made public, it was difficult to make comparisons between schools, and trends over the years were consequently not identifiable. Much of the reputation of a school, therefore, was based on its academic, sporting and cultural traditions and on the belief that it was doing a 'good' job. Since HMI reports were also not published, and LEAs did not evaluate the schools, parents had to base their judgments on their own impressions of a school and the oral tradition of neighbours and others with first-hand knowledge.

Such evidence of achievement is a very limited aspect of evaluation. But schools in the past were under no strong pressure to evaluate: their financial position was secure, pupil numbers were burgeoning, their catchment areas were fixed and parents were virtually compelled to accept the allocated school. Any suggestions of room for improvement were made discreetly. Today, however, with falling rolls and a Parents' Charter which gives parents the right to choose and urges them to do so after weighing up the quality of the programme, schools find themselves in competition with each other for pupils, and indeed for very survival. They are under pressure to be accountable to their more powerful governing bodies – and there is more to be accountable for. Advice showered on schools about whole school policies on issues as diverse as assessment, language across the curriculum and multiculturalism, demands response in the form of school policies articulated, implemented and monitored. New courses often have to meet the requirements of centrally-generated guidelines. Resources are being squeezed and management has to monitor practice to demonstrate that value for money is being obtained. Evaluation, too, is now seen as part of the cycle of continuous development, as important for raising awareness in the evolution of new policies, as for establishing the success of current practice.

What institutional development policy has been formulated?

I remember asking a primary headteacher friend, some years ago, if he had a policy on homework in his school. 'Yes', he replied, 'the policy is that every teacher has her own policy. This seems to work quite well.' Of course, as a parent with three children at the school told me, the policy meant that one of his children hardly ever had homework, a second was fully stretched every night, and the third child got homework occasionally. The parent confessed that it was difficult to explain to each child why his homework load varied, as all were equally motivated and successful at what they did.

Headteachers in primary schools saw themselves as buffers against external pressures rather than as leaders of a teaching team. Their objective was to create the conditions under which individual classroom teachers could get on with doing the job they had been trained to do. Of course, their skills might need to be enhanced in some respect to take account of the latest government advice on methods, but this could be done through exposure to an in-service course, and there was little need to plan consciously to develop a programme which had been successfully implemented by a stable, experienced staff over a lengthy period.

Management in secondary schools were equally unwilling to engage in whole-school curriculum planning, except in so far as timetabling was concerned. In the sixties and seventies energies were absorbed in coping with structural and logistical problems stemming from the reorganisation of secondary schools, the raising of the school leaving age, the bulge in adolescent numbers, the trend of staying on with its consequences for the traditional sixth form, and the introduction of systems of pastoral care and new examinations. There were poorly developed structures for consulting staff about these externally-generated changes at any level other than the subject or guidance team. Schools, in short, lacked a development policy, or a means of handling the increasingly diverse range of issues which society today expects schools to reflect in their curricular policies.

In the world of the eighties, the pressures which are leading schools to evaluate as a basis for development are also those which require schools to have an articulated policy on how change will be managed, and institutional practice developed. Such development inevitably means devising channels which will secure the participation in policy making of the whole staff, as a prelude to shared understandings about how to go about implementing them.

Staff development.

In a school system with little curriculum development and simple role structure, staff development was a strange and irrelevant concept. What was there to develop staff towards? In primary school the only promotion was to headteacher or infant mistress; in secondary, there were principal subject teachers and headteachers, but these jobs demanded experience rather than training. The introduction of a system of pastoral care in the late sixties created a new range of promoted posts which were also filled by untrained staff. Such staff development as occurred was by individual choice obtained outside the school and through LEA in-service programmes, and MEd or Open University courses.

Professional development was weakly conceptualised. Initial training was valued for the status it brought to the profession, rather than the skills it developed in the individual teacher. It was recognised that probation was necessary to consolidate initial training, but, with the exception of a few pilot schemes, little practical help was offered – for example, in the form of lighter timetables or specialist advice and support. Once probation was over, it was up to individual teachers, as professionals, to keep themselves up to date. Schools did not subscribe to educational publications, or send staff to conferences. Staffing needs were defined in terms of having enough bodies to fill classrooms to teach subjects. Schools today are under pressure to articulate and implement policies for staff development. In England and Wales staff appraisal looms as a means to establishing teacher competence and development needs which, if met, would also help the institution meet external expectations. School-based curriculum development is required to implement guidelines and to cope with the practical problems of integrating children with special educational needs, handling microcomputers, and offering a multicultural curriculum.

A wider variety of management tasks as coordinator of planning groups, resources, and specialised programmes (for example, for disruptive pupils) requires staff to develop greater expertise in cooperative activity. Staff are also involved in new roles with teacher education institutions. The return of adult learners to the classroom and the opening of community wings has meant that schools are dealing with a new and more sophisticated clientele than in the past. Teachers themselves, partly through a sense of professionalism and partly as a reflection of the competition for limited promotion opportunities, put discreet pressure on management to offer them support for development. Staff development, in short, is essential for the school to meet the wider responsibilities it is now expected to fulfil. The range of opportunities for staff development has widened, but the system still invests relatively little in this area.

How are resources managed and deployed?

Schools in the past used simple technology. In the mid forties, for example, I learned to write on a slate. At the end of the morning the teacher would go round the class with her water bottle dispensing drops so that we could clean our slates before the next exercise. There was a limited range of textbooks, some maps and posters from the 'cupboard', stuffed birds and animals from the days of 'object lessons', and of course, the blackboard. Towards the end of my primary school days we listened in to some broadcasts. In primary school, each teacher built up her own set of resources to suit her own curriculum, but these were not for sharing, even to the extent of telling other teachers what they consisted of. In secondary school, resources were requisitioned by the principal teacher of the subject and stored in the departmental cupboard. Much teaching was from the textbook, and the quality of explanations they offered was undoubtedly a significant factor in the success or failure of my own learning. The need for resources for teaching and learning is, to some extent, a reflection of the way in which the concept of the curriculum has itself changed. Certainly the range and quality of commercially-produced resources available to schools at reasonable cost has increased dramatically over the past thirty years. Printed materials, audio-visual aids, technological resources such as tape-recorders and video materials, as well as the minibus, provide teachers with the means to the provision of an enriched curriculum. Much of the centralised curriculum development effort sponsored by the Schools Council in the sixties and seventies was geared to developing resources for learning in connection with the raising of the school leaving age.

The fate of so many of these materials – stored in even less exalted places than school cupboards – highlights the general problem of how to harness resources to the delivery of better learning experiences for pupils. There is a widespread recognition today that suitable resources can result in a more varied curriculum, that they can facilitate individualised learning, and can be a powerful tool in translating abstract ideas into concrete terms – but the barriers to using them remain.

Headteachers and heads of department need to develop policies for the purchase, storing, and accessing of resources. In the best schools, purchase is a corporate decision reflecting a clear view of why the resources are required, and a satisfaction, stemming from evaluation (for example a curriculum analysis of printed materials), that the resources are likely to produce the effects their developers claim for them. Centralised storing is likely to be more helpful to the class teacher: a system can be evolved in which parents or ancillary staff can keep track of resources and draw attention to the strengths and weaknesses of acquisitions. Centralised storage can also be an effective way of monitoring usage. Similarly a central system can promote access in that teachers' requests can be handled in a systematic and even-handed manner. If more attention is paid to these aspects of the management of resources, teachers are more likely to feel supported in actually using them and in undertaking the considerable further work involved in adapting them for the specific purposes they have in mind. Resources are only a good investment if they are used, if their use is evaluated to establish how far they are proving effective with pupils, and if the evidence so obtained is fed back into in-school training so that all teachers can learn how to exploit their potential.

Policy issues in the next few years?

The point of this question, of course, is the future orientation of school management. How is the education system going to develop? What new demands can be anticipated? What kind of world should we be preparing young people for? How will the school have to change?

The school of the past was insulated from its environment. Contacts with parents and the world of commerce and industry were poorly developed. Few had good links with other schools even in the same catchment area although some of the more prestigious schools enjoyed a close, even incestuous, relationship with their neighbouring universities or colleges. At a time of full employment, and with student grants for all those who sought higher education, the school's role could be defined as ensuring pupils reached the tried and trusted academic standards of the past. But that world has gone, and schools have to justify their policies more vigorously than before and show that the courses they are offering provide pupils with the kinds of skills relevant for today's world of technology, environmental hazard and human need. Schools need allies in the outside world if their programmes are going to recruit adequately, and their staff need to be aware of the potential of new training courses in employment and higher education if they are to give useful guidance to school leavers. The quality of their own courses depends on their being kept up to date by staff trained in curriculum planning and evaluation, and sensitive to national and international trends. Time to foster these skills must be found. In short, management needs to develop a policy for innovating so that it can respond creatively to the pressures on schools.

Conclusion

It is inconceivable that any school management in Britain is not grappling with the kinds of issues discussed in this chapter. Some schools are more advanced than others in questioning the assumptions which underlie established practice, and finding new and more effective ways to meet the challenge implicit in defining the contemporary function of the school. The process involves conflict and uncertainty and demands high levels of professional skill and leadership. Innovation in education is extraordinarily difficult, but that is simply one of the problems to be recognised.

The issues dealt with in this chapter point to the curriculum as the focal point of the concerns of management in education. Quality in education boils down to quality in the curriculum. But before considering how to develop quality in the curriculum it is necessary to clarify the meaning of quality itself, and that is what is attempted in the next chapter.

2

Quality in Teaching

Quality in education can be discussed at a number of levels. One can consider the quality of the system as a whole at a particular point in time, comparing it with other national systems in respect of some aspect such as standards of attainment. Alternatively one can compare the performance of difference units within the system, for example, LEAs or schools, in terms of how successfully they implement particular policies, such as the provisions of the 1980 Education Act; or one can consider quality of performance of the individual teacher. While all these aspects are to some extent interrelated, the main focus here is on this last aspect.

The chapter begins with a definition of quality and some suggestions as to the sources of our concept of quality. One of the outcomes of the debate about accountability has been to clarify both the nature of the teacher's responsibilties for promoting learning, and the responsibilities of others in the education system to the teacher. The quality of the teacher's performance is likely to reflect the *match* of her skills to the teaching situation she is placed in (a reflection of management policies), and her *personal* capacities to deliver to a high standard. Evidence on a teacher's performance in the varied aspects of her role may be collected by a variety of techniques, and there are principles of evidence gathering and review that must be observed if interpretation and judgment of the evidence is to be soundly based. Such interpretation and judgment is invariably in terms of some notional standard of performance which an 'ideal' teacher could attain, or the 'best' teachers are currently attaining. Here, however, the purpose of studying quality is to understand it better, to clarify how it may be attained and to channel resources so that all teachers are helped to improve on their current level of performance and so to realise public expectations of the investment in the education system.

Defining quality in teaching

Pirsig (1976) relates quality to the Greek *arete* which means 'excellence of function' – the Greeks believing that every object, institution or individual had one special function to fulfil. On this definition the function of the teacher is seen here as to *plan and deliver a curriculum to her pupils, and to evaluate its success*. But it must be an *optimum* curriculum for the *individual* pupil, as a member (normally) of a class which contains pupils with a *range* of abilities and needs. My extended definition of quality in teaching is therefore:

> Planning, delivering and evaluating the optimum curriculum for the individual pupil in the context of a range of learners.

Of course this definition says nothing about the nature of the 'optimum' curriculum: different societies inevitably subscribe to different conceptions of personal development of pupils. Similarly our conception of 'good teaching' is culture relative.

Sources of our concept of quality in teaching

Travers' (1981) review of different criteria of 'good' teaching over the centuries concludes that different conceptions of 'good' have prevailed at different times. Socrates, the Sophists and the Savants of the medieval universities were 'good' because they attracted fee-paying students; by the 17th century teachers viewed themselves as managers of learning rather than holding themselves responsible for the learning itself; by the 19th century, as witness 'payment by results', securing learning was unmistakably the teacher's responsibility. Teachers today would view their role as 'enabling': most would accept the need to be able to demonstrate that they have provided all reasonable opportunities for a pupil to learn, both initially and by a variety of forms of remedial support, but many would resist the suggestion that they are to be held solely accountable for their pupils' learning.

All the great teachers have traditionally possessed three kinds of skill. First, charisma or the power of the magnetic personality. I had the good fortune to be taught English at school by such a person (Miller, 1970). Second, knowledge of the subjects to be taught, and high standards of correctness in grammar, punctuation and spelling. In 1986 the State of Texas, alarmed at the literacy level of its 210,000 teachers, required all to take tests of reading comprehension and to write an essay of 150 words (equivalent to what might be expected of typical eight-year-olds!) *Teaching Quality* (DES, 1983) drew attention to the gap between qualifications held and role in teaching in both primary and secondary schools. In primary schools weaknesses are apparent in specific curricular areas. HMI have observed, for example, that 'the most severe obstacle to the improvement of science in the primary school is that many existing teachers lack a working knowledge of elementary science appropriate to children of this age' (DES, 1978). In secondary schools a survey in England and Wales in 1977 found that one quarter of the teaching time was in the hands of teachers whose main subject of highest qualification was unrelated to the subject taught, and this lack of match was particularly evident in physics, religious education, metalwork, needlework, English and mathematics. The third skill of the teacher is variously referred to as pedagogic or 'craft skills'. These include skills of structuring knowledge for learning, questioning, developing and exploiting the potential of resources, managing group and individual learning. At one time it was assumed that only intending primary teachers needed to be trained in these skills but they are now recognised to require conscious development in teachers at every level.

Born teachers had charisma, but subject knowledge and craft skills were developed through training. The contemporary conception of quality adds to these the idea of the teacher as 'reflective practitioner' (Schon, 1983). Since the tasks facing teachers are constantly changing, teachers need continuously to be seeking ways to improve their practice. In the course of teaching, the teacher makes countless decisions as she 'reflects-in-action' on how to cope with the welter of interactions which she has to manage. Making conscious the nature of this professional knowledge by 'reflecting-on-action' subsequently can help the teacher see how she can make her practice more effective by being even better organised and knowing exactly how to motivate her pupils, and how to handle difficult pupils more sensitively. Quality in teaching, today, involves consciousness of the implications of decision-making, and the use of self-evaluation to guide planning to exploit the potential of teaching situations in a way which will offer richer learning experiences for pupils.

System factors affecting the quality of a teacher's work

A teacher's capacity to produce quality performance depends, to some extent, on decisions taken outwith her control. Central government is currently defining the curricular framework, and allocates the resources to be invested nationally. Factors such as staffing standards and finance for specific kinds of in-service may have direct implications for the quality of work a teacher can do. The LEA is immediately responsible for the allocation of resources, for establishing local curriculum development policies, for hiring staff, creating a climate of innovation and promoting staff development. The 'structure of opportunities' to enable staff to keep abreast of developments differs markedly between authorities, reflecting leadership priorities and situational factors such as size, personnel and remoteness from teacher training centres.

The school management team decides on the allocation of resources such as accommodation and equipment. It draws up the timetable, and takes decisions about grouping of pupils, class size, and (in secondary) the mix of classes a teacher will take, and for which aspects of the curriculum. The management team is also responsible for identifying and meeting staff development needs. It plays an important part, too, in determining how the curriculum is planned, and whether this is done by a 'course team' at secondary, or by teachers at a particular stage in primary, or is left to the individual teacher. Where planning is done jointly, there is collective responsibility for the decisions concerning what learning experiences are to be offered to pupils, how, when and by whom. But the individual teacher may then feel she is being asked to teach material about which she has misgivings, and that those who developed the ideas should also put them into practice.

A specific example can illustrate how a teacher's work may be influenced by decisions taken at a higher level. It is comfortably taken from a third world context because it illustrates one of the problems of developing quality in such systems, viz, the lack of reality of central government policies. In 1982 a new Minister of Education in Bangladesh announced that Arabic would be introduced in all primary one classes immediately to provide a third compulsory language (in addition to Bangla and English). Regional authorities were expected to implement the scheme, but teachers were untrained and there were no textbooks or other resources. Only the Islamic schools had a cadre of teachers who could teach the subject. The directive was passed down the line to the class teacher who naturally did nothing to implement the proposal. Ultimately the injunction was withdrawn with some loss of face, and with teachers concluding even more firmly than before that those who administered the system knew nothing of the problems of work at classroom level.

In Britain some teachers would no doubt regard the timescale set by government for introducing microcomputers, GCSE and YTS as exemplifying a similar failing.

Quality of performance of the classroom teacher

Two factors affect quality of performance: match and personal capacity. Match has already been discussed. Besides having appropriate subject knowledge of what she has to teach and adequate training for teaching pupils at the stage concerned, the teacher must also have sufficient appropriate resources of accommodation, teaching/learning materials, and time.

The better the match between what the teacher is asked to do and her ability to do it, the more easily differences in quality of performance can be explained by personal capacity factors. Personal capacity is the skill the teacher brings to the different aspects of her role, whether in contributing to planning decisions, the development of resource materials, delivery or evaluation of the curriculum. In the classroom it relates to her skill in the 'good teacher' role.

In *Human Characteristics and School Learning,* Ben Bloom (1978) illustrates personal capacity in his description of the coach helping the novice at tennis:

> 'The tutor first observes the student hitting several tennis balls in the serving position. He notes many details

in the way in which the server stands, holds the racket, swings, and hits the ball. What he is observing is where the learner is on some sequence in the learning of a particular task. What prerequisites has he already mastered and what does he still need to learn before he will reach some stage of mastery of the task under consideration?

He then begins his teaching by showing the student how he should hold the racket, stand, hit the ball and so on. He may break this down into several separable operations at first, but eventually he must bring them together into a single operation. This is the stage in which he is trying to provide the student with the *cues* as to what he is to learn. He may do this by talking to the student and explaining what he is to do, by using his own body to demonstrate what is expected, or by getting the student to stand, hold the racket, or swing in a particular manner. If the tutor is a very able one, he will provide a variety of cues to help the student understand what he is to do. The same task can be explained and/or illustrated in a variety of ways, and the tutor will search for the cues which will be best understood or grasped by the particular learner. The good tutor is likely to have a variety of ways of explaining or illustrating what is to be learned, and he will use one or more ways of presenting the cues which he believes will work best for the particular learner. He observes the student's responses to these cues, gives additional cues, or shifts the form of the cues until the student apparently grasps what he is to do.

Although it is relatively easy to observe the practice effects in a skill like serving a tennis ball, such practice or *participation* is necessary and must be present as a part of any kind of learning process – whether it be a highly abstract and complex cognitive type of problem solving, a less complex cognitive skill, or a more concrete psychomotor type of skill learning.

The good tutor recognises that the amount of participation or the amount of practice of the specific learning elements needed will vary from learner to learner. Some students will acquire it with a minimum of overt practice while others will need much more practice until they get it correct. Some learners can learn the entire operation in a few practice efforts while other learners must practice parts of the operation separately until they get each one to the proper level before they can practice the whole operation.

We further note that the tutor makes many little expressions of encouragement – usually when the student does something right or something nearly right. Sometimes these encouragements are expressed in words, sometimes in a smile, sometimes in a look or gesture. These encouragements seem to be most frequent at the beginning of the learning activity, and they appear to be reduced in frequency as the tutor notes the learner responding with smiles, gestures, nods, or monosyllables as he (the learner) does something that seems to work and he believes is good; or with frowns, grimaces, or expressions of dismay, as he does something that he regards as wrong or ineffective. The good tutor varies the types of encouragement or *reinforcement* with the learning situation, the stages in the learning activity, and the learner. Furthermore, he attempts to create a situation (as suggested above) in which the learner becomes his own source of reinforcement. Essentially, the tutor manages the student's learning to ensure that the learner secures the necessary *reinforcement* or *rewards* to motivate his participation and perseverance in the learning as well as to signal when parts of the learning are going well.

At various stages in learning, the tutor checks on the learner to note what he has accomplished and to determine where or when he needs additional correction and support. This is what we have termed *feedback* and *correction*. Here the tutor may alter the instruction to help the learner over particular difficulties. He may get the learner to practice a particular aspect of the learning to strengthen particular correct procedures or to eliminate specific incorrect ones. He may also alter the reinforcements to make them more appropriate to the learner.'

Bloom shows how the coach first *assesses* the novice's current level of performance and then by means of *cues,* providing *practice opportunities* for the student so that he can participate first-hand in the learning, offering *reinforcement* or *rewards* to motivate and encourage persistence, and providing *feedback* or *correction* he helps the student achieve higher standards of performance. While the emphasis in Bloom's description is on the pedagogic skill of the coach, the perceptive reader will not have failed to notice what is implicit in the account: the match between the coach's high level of skill (subject expertise) and the learning situation he is working in. However, Bloom is not implying that the pupil of such a teacher is guaranteed to learn: simply that the process of learning is facilitated by coaches who model such qualities and skills and interact with pupils in the ways described.

Studying quality in teaching

The definition of quality of teaching outlined earlier, highlighted the range of tasks involved prior, during and subsequent to the face-to-face encounter with pupils in the classroom. Teachers' work involves activities, hidden from pupils and parents, in the organisation of the school, development of teaching materials, assessing pupils' work, meeting with psychologists and health visitors, etc., as well as engaging in the kinds of activities of Bloom's tennis coach. The quality with which these other aspects of his work are tackled is likely to influence, and in some cases determine, the quality of the face-to-face encounter. At the same time, some of these activities, such as the preparation of resource materials and the setting of valid examination questions, are likely to be more directly related to the quality of the learning experience enjoyed by the pupil than others.

The study of teaching quality has been bedevilled by focusing on limited criteria of effectiveness. It is inappropriate to make judgments of effectiveness until we have better descriptions of how teachers actually undertake the range of tasks associated with the job. In studying quality, therefore, there are two questions to consider: which teachers to focus on, and which aspects of teacher behaviour to collect evidence on.

Relevant contrasts between teachers

Focusing on outstanding teachers alone – however these are identified – is unlikely to clarify what makes the difference between them and more typical performers. Nor is a straight contrast between 'the best' and 'the worst' likely to help.

Lyle Spencer (1983) emphasises the importance of contrasting the performance of outstanding and typical professionals in a field so that differences become clearer. The technique he has developed for doing this involves obtaining evidence on a wide range of criteria of performance effectiveness which might include, for teachers, hard data such as teaching materials produced and pupils' examination results, and ratings by management, peers and pupils. Interviews with superior and average performers focus on how they handled the most critical situations relevant for 'success' in the job, and the skills and competencies they used in the job itself. Spencer highlights the importance of 'soft skills' of critical thinking (ability to make critical distinctions or inferences, cite data to support positions, and to reconcile conflicting data pro and con inferences) and accurate empathy (accurate hearing of the content, meaning and feeling of what another person is saying) as crucial for differentiating among professionals in civil service, business and the armed forces in USA.

One study which focuses on the differences in performance of outstanding and typical teachers was carried out by Moskowitz (1978) who studied eleven foreign language teachers. He found that outstanding teachers and their students used the foreign language more than typical foreign language teachers and their students. They controlled pupils more indirectly by smiles, approving nods and frowns rather than by verbal reprimands, and praised, joked and personalised questions significantly more and criticised pupils less than typical teachers. But these results can offer no more than an indication of what general differences might exist.

Collecting evidence on teacher quality

The relevant questions here involve asking what evidence, collected by what means, by whom, and for what purpose? Four kinds of evidence may be collected on a teacher's performance:

1 *documentary evidence* i.e. the materials he has prepared, test questions set, record system, letters to parents, etc.;
2 *observational evidence* either first-hand by watching the teacher at work, or second-hand by interviewing him, or asking

those who have been in his presence while he worked about his performance;

3 *achievement evidence* i.e. what his pupils achieve as a result of being in his class for a period of time in terms of workbooks completed, examination results, attitude to the subject, intellectual and practical skills; and

4 *factual evidence* i.e. on such matters as attendance, lateness and degree of participation in extra-curricular activities.

In view of what was said earlier about the range of tasks which teachers undertake as part of their work, the first criterion in collecting evidence is ensuring that a *comprehensive* range of *relevant* evidence is obtained. Who decides what is 'relevant' may itself be problematical, but both the individual teacher and those concerned with the study of quality could define the evidence they regard as relevant for any discussion of quality of performance. Teachers might be asked to prepare a dossier of their work over a year to do justice to the range of activities in which they have been engaged, and to indicate which of that work they consider to have been most successful and why.

The second criterion is the manner in which evidence is collected and by whom. Systematic, objective and disinterested methods are essential to quality evaluation. Some evidence may well be collected by delegating the task to one person (for example considering the factual evidence on a teacher's year in school). Where observational evidence is to be collected it is important that several informed observers are involved. Observers should reflect different perspectives but be agreed on what behaviours they are interested in observing, thus increasing the reliability of their collective account of the teacher's practice, and so maximising the prospects of a fair and balanced view of that performance emerging. These multiple viewpoints are equally essential when interviewing a teacher about his work and in reviewing the range of evidence which has been collected in the process of evaluation.

Judging quality

Quality of judgments and judgments of quality are interrelated. Quality of judgments will reflect the extent to which the principles of collecting evidence outlined above have been observed, the training provided to those who make judgments and their skill (and motivation) in weighing up and interpreting the available evidence. Given these conditions the quality of judgments made on individual teachers is likely to be sound. The judgment of an individual's quality is likely to highlight strengths and weaknesses, and to provide a spur to individual development, provided the judgment is accepted as valid. On a broader canvas these judgments, if collected at appropriate points in the career cycle of teachers, could help define standards for initial teacher training, for levels of competence to be achieved within probation and for promotion to a senior post. In short, they can aid managers of the education service to understand the quality of the teaching force and where resources might be best invested to improve teachers' skills.

Conclusion

This chapter began by defining quality of teaching in relation to planning, delivering and evaluating the curriculum for the individual learner. It has ended by suggesting how quality of individual performance may be defined and evaluated, issues which are explored further in Chapter 7. But school management is primarily concerned with improvement of the curriculum. We now turn to how we can improve the quality of this aspect within the functioning of schools.

3

School Quality: Expectations and Responsibilities

As the last chapter indicated, accountability for the quality of a school programme cannot be placed exclusively at one level of the system. At the same time there can be no doubt that the headteacher and the management team can, and do, enormously influence the effectiveness of a school. Indeed HMI, in *Ten Good Schools* (DES, 1977), identified the quality of leadership of the headteacher as the single most important factor in the success of the schools studied.

Government has prescribed a range of professional duties for headteachers to undertake in the pursuit of quality, but recent observational evidence on headteachers at work indicates that they have other priorities. Headteachers themselves need staff development to undertake the kinds of tasks government expect them to do, but headteachers can still get close to the expectations held by groups and individuals who constitute their clients – HMIs, LEAs, other educational institutions and community interests – and their customers (pupils and their parents). How these groups define quality can promote awareness of the gap between what is wanted, and what is being achieved in the curriculum, and can provide a spur to improvement. This chapter addresses five issues:

- Government expectations and headteachers' current activities.
- Clients' views of quality.

- Customers' views of quality.
- Reviewing the implemented curriculum.
- Bringing expectations and reality closer.

Headteachers' work and government expectations

Recent government reports and the 1986 Audit Commission have spelled out a number of criteria for better management of schools. Headteachers, besides demonstrating appropriate personal qualities such as good humour, a sense of proportion and dedication to the job should demonstrate skills of:

1 Communicating the school's specific educational aims (for example, via prospectus and reports) to governors, staff, pupils and parents.
2 Effective management of teaching staff and pupils, materials and other resources including finance.
3 Systematic curriculum review leading to the introduction of policies for multiculturalism, integration of pupils with special educational needs, microcomputers, assessment.
4 Evaluation including review of subject programmes, schemes of work.
5 Performance appraisal and development of teachers.

In addition to these skills management styles should emphasise power sharing, and devolution of responsibility to staff who work together as a team.

In her study of headteachers at work, Valerie Hall and her colleagues (1986) found that many of these aspects were virtually ignored. Classroom supervision, performance appraisal, departmental evaluation and systematic curriculum review, for example, were rarely carried out. Their single day observations of fifteen heads showed considerable individual diversity, but their daily work was fragmented, people-intensive, and encompassed a range of tasks.

> 'Teaching emerged as the longest sustained activity for many headteachers and formal scheduled meetings constituted a

> low proportion of the job. The majority of the head's activities were interpersonal, predominantly with individuals and groups within the school, although they gave vastly different emphasis to the importance of building and maintaining interpersonal relations and motivating staff. They differed substantially in their levels of involvement in the tasks to be carried out as a result of their contrasting interpretations of the head's role. In general, they spent more time on teaching activities than on "leading professional" matters of curriculum and other educational policy; more time on "operations" and "human management" than on "educational policy"; and about ten per cent of their time daily, in the school on "external management" matters. Routine administration dominated the time spent within the "operations management" category. Pupil issues claimed just over half of their "human management" time.' (p. 205)

If there is to be a closer match between government expectations and what is actually achieved, headteachers will need to review how they spend their time, consult staff more systematically, develop professional skills of planning and monitoring, and learn to review their own effectiveness. In the longer term there are implications for selection and training for headship (see Chapter 7). But headteachers can raise their own level of awareness about how successfully their schools are perceived by establishing the expectations held by clients and customers nationally and locally, and by having these discussed by their colleagues as a stimulus to thinking about where improvements might be made.

Quality of schools and the expectations of clients

Clients are all those groups who have an indirect or second-level interest in the quality of the school programme. They include government, LEAs, other educational institutions and local and national commercial and community interests. Each will define quality in its own terms: government may be concerned with curricular breadth, and industrialists with standards of attainment in basic skills, while a community group may be more concerned with aspects of pupil behaviour, such as participation in community service or vandalism. A headteacher should know the expectations of clients, and consider how far his school is meeting them, and how far it could or should do so.

HMI reports

Criteria of quality being employed by HMI can be deduced from two sources: published reports of inspections of over 200 educational establishments per year and surveys of practice. John Pearce (1986) has suggested that HMI employ six criteria in evaluating schools:

1 *Plant:* HMI observe the adequacy-for-purpose and condition of educational buildings and grounds in relation to the demands made on them by curriculum and the needs of pupils, with the well-justified belief that shabby buildings invite their users to treat them shabbily.

2 *Match:* HMI are closely interested in how well the work that pupils are asked to do, is aligned to their aptitudes and abilities (in all their variety). In particular HMI look for evidence of firm expectations by teachers at both ends of the range of ability as well as across it.

3 *Pedagogy:* HMI expect the school to engage its pupils, at all levels of age and ability, as active participants in their own learning. They are relatively uninterested in teaching in any performative sense: their concern is with what the pupil does, rather than with the teacher. They look for learning that is active, oral and questioning rather than passive, silent and receptive. They seek real problem-solving in place of token exercises and formal drills. These priorities rest on large-scale observation of pupil performance: HMI have seen quite enough good work of this order to be confident that the demand they make is reasonable.

4 *Progression:* HMI seek patterns of work planned to yield a real movement, that the pupil is regularly made aware of, from week to week, term to term, year to year, school to school, in an overall curriculum where balance and breadth make the progression found in each area coherent and ordered.

5 *Professionalism:* HMI expect teachers to do the jobs they are appointed to do: they are impatient of heads of department who do not manage or lead, appointments carrying emolument but not duties, status but not responsibility, structure but not meaning.

6 *Climate:* HMI have very sensitive antennae for the quality of relationships in school, between pupil and pupil, teacher and teacher, as well as between teacher and class. They view a supportive and reassuring climate of good order as significant, not only for the personal and social education of the pupils, but for the delivery of an effective curriculum. (pp. 138–9)

The dominant theme, Pearce suggests, is the relationship between 'match' and 'pedagogy'. HMI are specially critical of 'teaching for the middle' – the use of undifferentiated, whole-class methods and materials with classes set up and defined as mixed ability. This practice fails the test of 'match' for the most and least able alike, and because whole class methods lead to teacher-centred instruction it fails the test of 'pedagogy'.

In their *Survey of Primary Education in England and Wales* (DES, 1978) HMI compared the level of tasks set in different curricular areas to the standard of work the children were doing or had completed:

> 'A reasonably satisfactory match was recorded when the tasks presented to children were related to their existing skills and knowledge, when there was evidence of progression in the work and when there was evidence of the acquisition of further skill, information or understanding. When work was presented at the right level of difficulty children were normally confident and not afraid to make occasional errors which they regarded as a stimulus for further effort; in these circumstances children displayed a sense of purpose in their work and appeared to enjoy the challenge of the increasing though realistic, demands made upon them.' (pp. 80–1)

The findings indicate that, where work was not reasonably matched to children's capabilities, it was insufficiently demanding. Science was an aspect where matching was found least often ('children were not sufficiently challenged in over two-thirds of all groups' (p. 82)). While matching was reasonably successful in language, mathematics and physical education, in other subject areas there was a widespread tendency to underestimate the capacities of all groups of children.

The survey listed a set of curricular items, each of which was found to occur individually in at least eighty per cent of the classes surveyed. Some of these, such as reading practice with a main reading scheme, took place in every seven-year-old class. But no single item relating to science fell into this category and it was also not possible to specify a range of content being covered within history and geography When all items listed for all subjects were considered together 'less than a third of the seven-year-old classes, about a fifth of the nine-year-old classes, and a quarter of the eleven-year-old classes included all the activities' (pp. 79–80). The report, therefore, highlighted how curriculum planning was being undertaken on an apparently individualised basis in each school and the inconsistency of coverage of what were widely regarded as important curricular areas.

Since 1981, HMI reports on individual schools have been published. The criteria on which schools and teachers are judged change over the years, but a recent analysis of reports on secondary schools by staff in one education authority in Scotland, found that the elements of work which were most closely scrutinised comprised departmental management and teaching and learning.

HMI scrutinised departmental policies on assessment, discipline, learning difficulties, language, resource use/management and homework, the relationship between such policies and whole school policies, policy evolution and communication to members of the department, probationers and student teachers. Implementation and monitoring of policy by the principal teacher and identification of related staff development needs were also studied.

In teaching and learning, HMI were interested in the role of the subject as the vehicle for the development of a range of skills and attitudes, the quality and range of learning activities offered to pupils, programmes of work (in terms of the interest and motivation through direct involvement in the learning process of pupils, and the integration of fieldwork and audio/visual resources in the syllabus), differentiation (i.e. the extent of individualising the curriculum, and of cooperative or team teaching), progression between stages (for example, primary to secondary, and across the stages within secondary – progression being defined in terms of skills, concepts and learning activities rather than simply in terms of content), use of an appropriate range of methods, and resources. HMI were interested in the quality of home-produced resources such as worksheets in terms of layout, amount of text, standard of diagrams and other graphics, and accessibility of language to the range of pupils, and in the extent to which visual resources help to illustrate the ideas or concepts being taught.

There is an agenda of issues here for a head to consider, with his staff, both for preparing themselves to cope with an inspection more confidently and also as guidelines for developing their own practice.

Monitoring studies

The monitoring of standards of achievement in Britain has been practised since the end of the Second World War. The aim today is to provide information on what pupils know, and can do, at selected stages in their education in a range of curricular areas. Monitoring also aims to provide comparison of standards of performance over time (by repeating tests at intervals where possible) and to investigate ways in which the findings can be used nationally by education authorities, by curriculum developers and by teachers, to evaluate and develop educational policy and to improve learning and teaching.

Surveys have been undertaken nationally by the Assessment of Performance Unit (APU) in England and Wales and as part of the Scottish Education Department's (SED) Assessment of Achievement Programme (AAP) in Scotland. Some local authorities and individual schools also undertake monitoring programmes, using objective tests. Monitoring has been undertaken in only selected areas of the curriculum notably in language and mathematics, modern languages and science. Home economics and technical subjects have also been surveyed in Scotland. Attempts to monitor in aesthetic areas have been abandoned.

Survey reports were too technical and dull in the past to be widely read by heads and school staff, and there were problems in relating general trends to specific school practice. But monitoring is clarifying some aspects of what is being achieved nationally. Piloting gives teachers experience of new approaches to assessment, and stimulates thinking about the objectives, content and methods of the curriculum.

In his recent analysis of the APU's Language Testing Programme, Geoffrey Thornton (1986) suggested that the surveys had thrown new light on the nature of the interaction between a language task that a pupil might be asked to undertake, and his resultant level of performance. But to improve pupil achievement teachers 'must know something about language itself, how it works and how it achieves its effects', and this implies better initial training and more intensive in-service training to develop this aspect of subject expertise in the teacher. Thornton suggests that headteachers have a key role in helping school staff translate survey implications into practice – by requiring reviews of the school language syllabus, by ensuring that there are consequent changes in classroom practice (for example, in the amounts and kinds of writing asked for), and by making sure that parents are kept informed. The headteacher or head of department can check that books and materials requisitioned reflect the principles of language learning endorsed by the surveys. There are also implications for the deployment of subject specialists in secondary schools, to ensure that less proficient writers (mainly boys) who gravitate into option classes such as Craft, Design and Technology and science are offered most help in improving their writing performance. From the AAP maths survey have materialised attractive folios for schools setting out succinctly the background to the studies, summary results of achievement data on the aspect (for example, decimals) tested, and 'some issues for debate', such as:

- Are vulgar fractions conceptually too difficult even for thirteen-year-olds?
- How can we give more practice in estimation and approximation?

Monitoring clarifies the criteria for evaluating school programmes. HMI will expect to find that the headteacher and his staff are aware of the nature of the deabte about quality stemming from the analysis of the survey results, and are reviewing their policies in the light of this.

LEAs

Although LEAs have management responsibilities for schools, they have not, until very recently, viewed their responsibilities as extending to the formulation of curricular policies. John Pearce (1986) suggested that, in the past, 'improvement' in the curriculum was achieved through advisers working with individual subject teachers and headteachers to develop resources or putting on ad hoc in-service courses. In the seventies a number of LEAs set up review bodies to prepare curriculum guidelines, but these were not mandatory, and teachers could assert their professional right to do things 'their way' and ignore official policy. Authorities could see the emergence of 'responsive' and 'unresponsive' primary schools and subject departments, and yet feel powerless to intervene.

The level of LEA support available to a headteacher for curriculum review will reflect the extent to which an authority is responding to central government expectations. The headteacher can seek clarification of overall and specific curriculum policies and available resources, and feed this into the thinking process of the school. He can seek to involve advisory staff directly in assisting him, and heads of subject departments, to develop policies, and to offer related in-service support and advice. The adviser is also the outsider best placed to supplement school-based attempts to improve the quality of teaching of individual members of staff. Although evidence from USA (Bridges, 1985) suggests that incompetent teachers rarely improve, the adviser can effect transfer or secondment which may be the stimulus a teacher needs to find renewed motivation for his work.

Other educational bodies

Schools have a range of other clients in the education system which include other schools to whom pupils will transfer, further and higher education, colleges of education, and educational research teams. Transfer could be smoothed if reports communicated between institutions were soundly based, and if students were adequately prepared for the demands of the stage to which they are proceeding. Development of study skills (see Selmes, 1986) and opportunities for counselling and career guidance based on realistic up-to-date information on developments in post-school education will affect pupils' choice and their ability to cope with new demands. Headteachers may regard invitations to participate in selection of students for initial teacher training courses, or placing requests for students by colleges of education, and requests for access to children and to staff in connection with research projects, as impositions and hassle, but viewed positively they can provide access to new ideas and promote staff development. Staff involved in the selection programme for admission to teacher training at my college, have spoken enthusiastically about the insights into assessment the system has offered, and the professional development that has occurred through working as partners with colleagues from schools and colleges.

Many of the new teacher training courses approved by the Council for National Academic Awards (CNAA) have involved systematic efforts to brief teachers on ways to support and assess students on placement, thus enhancing awareness of quality of teaching. Collaborative research projects such as that described by Christine De Luca (a teacher) and Harry Black (a researcher) who jointly (1979) developed a modular diagnostic-based programme for first-year pupils in geography, bring new ways of thinking about curriculum and assessment into school programmes and can have a powerful spin-off in terms of enthusiasm and staff development.

Other community, commercial and industrial interests

A school's quality is defined by its clients in the local, national and international community. The headteacher cannot ignore the different and often conflicting expectations held by community representatives from different social and ethnic backgrounds, and the commercial and industrial sectors. Representatives of these interests have expectations that curricular materials will be scrutinised for sex stereotyping and ethnocentricism, while the community expects schools to be in the front line in the fight against AIDS, drug abuse and soccer violence. Employers have criticised standards of attainment in literacy and numeracy as long as public education has been provided: the Bullock Report (DES, 1975) quoted the 1921 Newbolt Report as expressing surprise and disappointment that 'our young employees are so hopelessly deficient in their command of English'. But to meet such criticisms depends upon being clear about the demands of the particular linguistic tasks employers have in mind.

The Technical and Vocational Education Initiative (TVEI) has required schools to devise courses which meet such criteria as:

- preparing the student for particular aspects of employment and for adult life in a society liable to rapid change;
- encouraging initiative, problem solving abilities and other aspects of personal development;
- avoiding sex stereotyping in curricular choice; and
- providing appropriate planned work experience.

Oliver Fulton (1987) suggests that the main effect of TVEI lies in the personal and social development and motivation of young people, who were not much interested in the traditional curriculum and methods by which it was taught.The extension of this scheme to all schools from 1986 offers heads and teaching staff a model for developing curricula to meet the expectations of clients in the local community.

Quality of schools and the expectations of customers

A school's customers are children and their parents. Children like going to school, at least at primary level, because of the exciting social opportunities it offers, and the ready access to friends. Neville Bennett and his colleagues (1984) pointed out how children cheerfully cooperate with their teachers even in doing the routine, rather boring, tasks which comprise the bulk of the curriculum, grumbling only when they are unclear as to what is expected of them or when the tasks are beyond their competence. At secondary level their attitude to the curriculum reflects the course they are following: surveys in Scotland such as *The Best Years?* (Hughes, 1984) and *Tell Them From Me* (Gow and McPherson, 1980) indicate that those on certificate courses will passively accept monotonous teaching while non-certificate pupils play up, 'act stupid', and leave as soon as they are of age.

Pupils do recognise the effort and commitment of teachers. There is also evidence that they have clear views about teacher quality. They respect teachers who do not bore them and are not martinets, who do not put on acts but are themselves, express genuine anger when this is appropriate, do not waste time insisting on unreal standards of neatness and uniformity, do not shout at them or show rudeness, do not have favourites, are conscientious in setting and marking homework, do not attempt to be as friendly in class as they are in social situations away from the classroom,are humorous, can admit that they are wrong, do not treat them 'like kids', know their names and are fair and treat them as individuals. Pupils' perception of the quality of a school reflects its respect for them. This respect may be expressed in terms of whether they can learn what they want to learn and what they find meaningful to learn, the ways in which teachers consider their interests and views on the quality of courses and the treatment they receive.

The Parents' Charter requires schools (and LEAs) to provide parents with more information about policies, practice and achievements than in the past. Indeed the 1981 Education Act on special educational needs gave parents rights going beyond anything previously offered under existing educational legislation. Parents have a statutory right to be fully involved as partners with professional staff in assessing a child's special needs and compiling a 'statement' of these needs and required provision, although Rogers (1987) has shown how LEAs have evaded this clause.

Parents, of course, display a wide range of attitudes to education, but as a group their expectations are rising. They are more sophisticated and expect better quality information about the objectives of the school programme, the rationale for curriculum policies such as option arrangements, the resources being used, and the results (particularly in respect of external examinations) being achieved. They expect to be consulted by staff about, for example, school rules and dress, and this means negotiation rather than diktat by the head. Parents voting with their feet can, of course, reflect school stereotyping. But this simply highlights the public relations challenge facing a headteacher who wants to convince parents that the school he runs offers better value than one that has a supposedly 'better' reputation

The school response : reviewing the implemented curriculum

It is the headteacher's responsibility to know what expectations are held of schools in general, and his school in particular, and to present these in a constructive way to his staff. One

Stage 1 Getting Started

1 Decide whether this method is appropriate for your needs

2 Consult the staff

3 Appoint a school coordinator

Stage 2 Initial Review

1 Plan the initial review

2 Collect information

3 Survey staff opinion

4 Identify priority areas

Stage 3 Specific Review

1 Plan the specific reveiw

2 Identify present policy/practice

3 Check on its implementation and effectiveness

4 Draw up recommendations for development

Stage 4 Action for Development

1 Check on the implications of the development plan

2 Decide what INSET opportunities should be made available

3 Action

Stage 5 Overview and Restart

1 Decide whether the changes should be made permanent

2 Decide whether and how to restart

3 Restart

Figure 3.1 The Five Stages of the Institutional Review and Development Process implication is his need to establish the quality of the curriculum the school is currently delivering. This means examining the relationship between school policy and practice at three levels viz:

- the whole school level;
- the departmental level;
- the individual teacher in the classroom.

At the whole school level, school-based curriculum review can provide evidence on the extent to which national and local curricular policies are being put into practice. Malcolm Skilbeck introduced the idea in the mid-seventies; since then many LEAs have produced checklists of issues which school staff should consider systematically. These checklists are daunting to contemplate, especially for staff unused to such deliberations, and headteachers often lack the management skills to implement such a review. Help with management has been provided in the Guidelines for Review and Internal Development in Schools (GRIDS) project (McMahon, 1984) in the form of identifying a specific target to focus on, and following out a sequence of steps for tackling it. The steps involved are outlined in Figure 3.1.

An external consultant can often be an important ally for the head in getting the review process under way, and ensuring that the momentum is maintained, a point discussed more fully in Chapter 6.

At departmental level subject advisers from the LEA can assist in the review process, but it is important that the criteria applied to current practice reflect whole school policies, and that issues are shared with senior management. However, it is at classroom level that the headteacher can see the reality of what pupils are experiencing as a curriculum. As Pearce (1986) remarks, 'the headteacher who is serious about managing the quality of teaching is observing lessons, and many of them, all the time' (p. 208), focusing less on the performance of the teacher, and more on what he is getting his pupils to do, and with what level of success.

Bringing expectations and reality closer

Studying what teachers do can illuminate where improvements are needed. A headteacher who is sensitive to external expectations, or the context in which his school is operating, can use that evidence to identify priorities for development. He can exploit evidence of the enthusiasm and skills of staff, and devise effective strategies to motivate the apathetic. The range in expectations of clients and customers of schools implies more conscious decision making, the development of a rationale for policy which is defensible because it is principled, and better planning of the structure and content of the curriculum and the resources through which it will be delivered.

Better planning means clarifying objectives and contextualising a programme in relation to its consumers. Planning involves developing awareness in staff of what they have to teach and why, ensuring that they have the resources to deliver it, and monitoring practice to ensure that the plans are feasible and produce the expected gains in learning.

Conclusion

This chapter began by contrasting the management responsibilities government was laying on headteachers with observational evidence as to where headteachers' priorities currently lie. It has been argued that if headteachers are to fulfil government expectations they must be more sensitive to the definition of quality held by their clients and customers. Exploring these expectations involves creating channels with local community interests, attending conferences and meetings, and above all keeping up to date with the volume of government and other school-related publications on educational matters. Headteachers need to invest in professional literature, summarising and sometimes simplifying reports and policy statements for the staff as a whole.

Before the headteacher can interpret these conflicting expectations he needs to secure the support of his colleagues in thinking through the curriculum appropriate to the context in which they operate. The first step is to find out what policies the school *currently* operates, and the quality of teaching and learning being delivered by staff. It is the head's responsibility to set the process in motion through review and direct observation of teachers at work. External consultants may be required to guide the direction of development, but the head has to create the climate in which discussion can take place, and it becomes acceptable to talk of improvements in teaching as being necessary and possible. In the next chapter we discuss ways of planning these improvements.

Before concluding, however, a parallel with commerce and industry which has underlain much of this chapter should be made explicit. Tom Peters and Nancy Austin (1984) suggest that long-term excellence in business organisations reflects four factors:

- meeting the expectations of clients;
- superior service to the customer;
- full use of the abilities of every member of staff;
- constant innovation.

The element which links these factors together is *leadership*. At the heart of leadership, as stated by Austin and Peters in MBWA – *Management by Wandering About* – where the top executive eschews his office, is visible, active, makes direct contact with clients and staff, listens to what they have to say, and acts on their complaints. Successful headteachers exemplify such characteristics as 'vision, energy, empathy, persistence, passion, attention to detail, a picture of the goal!'

There are interesting parallels between education and business, and this study which provides many examples of the conception of new products and their successful marketing could give headteachers much food for thought as to how to go about planning.

4

Quality of Planning

In the previous chapter it was argued that the stimulus to improvement of the quality of the curriculum is an awareness of the gap between expectations and achievements. Improvement involves thinking harder about what schools are trying to achieve, and how they can provide their pupils with appropriate learning experiences to realise their objectives. In short it means paying more attention to curriculum planning.

Much of the curriculum planning which is changing the face of British education is being undertaken by agents of central government such as the Secondary Examinations Council and the Council for National Academic Awards. These bodies have established frameworks and criteria for courses. Schools and colleges which wish to offer programmes leading to their qualifications are required to submit proposals which reflect the conditions laid down. This chapter is concerned initially with planning at this macro level; subsequently issues at the school and class teacher level are reviewed more briefly.

The quality of a plan can be established ultimately only if it leads to improvements in practice, that is, *if it works*. But plans themselves can be evaluated in terms of the quality of their rationale, the extent to which they meet such desiderata as coherence and progression and feasibility. How sound are the frameworks currently being devised? What are the implications of more centralised planning for the freedom of the school, the department and the subject teacher? Which aspects of planning are best undertaken centrally and which locally? And how should planning actually be managed?

The meaning of planning

Planning means all the stages in the preparation of a curriculum before it is actually used with the target group. It is a process which includes empirical research, deliberation and a try out of materials to be used in teaching and learning, and briefing of those who are actually to teach the course itself. There are three main aspects:

Development of a framework for a course

The framework is determined by such factors as the objectives of a course, the components or subjects to be studied, its length and how the time is to be allocated to units of learning. Frameworks may be laid down by central government (GCSE is an example), and schools wishing to present for the certificate have to produce proposals which conform to its specifications. This aspect of planning results in the production of written statements of intent, promises of what the curriculum will try to achieve and the nature of the learning experiences through which delivery will be undertaken.

Development of resources for implementing the framework

A range of materials for teaching pupils, developing their understanding and assessing their learning have to be devised if the plan is to be made operational. In addition to textbooks and printed materials, a wide range of audio-visual resources, environmental sources, and artefacts may be made available: identifying such resources, adapting them for the specific context in which they are to be used, and assembling them for classroom use are important aspects of 'fleshing out' a curriculum planning statement into a course ready for delivery.

Briefing of staff who have to implement the course

A course may be delivered only by the member of staff who planned it, but an increasingly common situation is where a course team is given responsibility. If pupils in 'parallel classrooms' are to be given similar learning experiences to achieve the objectives of the course, it is essential to ensure that all those teaching the course understand what is to be achieved, exploit the potential of the resources, and manage the learning towards a common end.

Planning is a cyclical process. The same course is never offered twice, and there is scope for development in the light of experience of teaching the course: monitoring of delivery, and reflection on the contribution made by different elements such as the amount of information to be absorbed, the appeal of student-centred activities, and the achievements of pupils can guide further development of the course towards an improved Mark II version.

Principles of planning

Planning involves predicting what pupils will need or want to learn, and devising a series of learning experiences which will provide an opportunity for the required or desired learning to take place. It is principled when planners approach the task, having regard to a number of key issues which they tackle systematically. The issues are logically interrelated and include:

1 Being clear about the objectives to be pursued: the derivation of objectives should reflect an analysis of the nature of competent performance in the area with which the course is concerned. In vocational training, objectives would derive from an analysis of the skills required to do the job. Objectives derive from the *rationale* for the course, that is, the reason why we need the course at all.

2 Knowing the characteristics of the entering pupils: the learning experiences previously successfully encountered, and the range of skills and attitudes likely to be displayed by those enrolling, can determine how the course is initially structured, thus ensuring good 'articulation' or linkage to previous courses.

3 Identifying the essential knowledge and skill areas which pupils must master if the objectives of the course are to be attained, and ensuring that this is given appropriate emphasis in the learning activities which are devised.

4 Structuring the course to ensure that a coherent experience is provided, while building in flexibility so that the principle of choice can be respected, and new knowledge areas readily introduced. Structuring relates to the deployment of time available for the course. Issues in structuring include the

balance between 'core' and 'optional' elements, the length of the unit of teaching/learning (for example, a thirty-hour module for each block), articulation between units, and coherence across the course as a whole.

5 Within each unit offering learning experiences, which make progressively greater demands on the pupil, and which are resourced with an appropriate range of learning approaches and materials.

6 Devising reliable and valid forms of assessment of pupil learning, feeding the evidence collected back to the pupil, and providing adequate opportunities for overcoming difficulties or mistakes.

7 Defining for both teacher and pupils what counts as 'success' on the course, both in terms of the activities to be undertaken and the standards of attainment to be reached, and pointing up the connection between objectives, learning experiences and assessment demands.

8 Recognising the demands a course will place on teachers (in terms of delivery), ensuring that these are feasible and building in various forms of support including the time for development work, briefings and follow up.

These principles imply that curriculum planning should be research-based, should reflect a theory of curriculum design which is informed by evidence on how pupils learn, and be deliberative in that it beings a wide range of perspectives to bear, and results in value issues being made explicit.

Planning models

The idea of a research-based, systematically planned approach to curriculum design underlies many of the curriculum development projects of the sixties. These projects focused on the subject rather than on the curriculum as a whole. Bruner's *Man: A Course of Study* (MACOS) (1965) for example, attempted to give pupils between the ages of nine and thirteen the beginnings of a social scientist's way of thinking – a curiosity about behaviour, and tools and a conceptual framework for organising and reflecting about experience. An impressive collection of materials (literary and audio-visual) supported the course, teacher guides were prepared, and attendance by school staff at a workshop was a precondition of the purchase of materials. The course presented a considerable challenge to teachers both intellectually – since few of the teachers working with MACOS were trained in the social sciences – and in terms of role, since the materials were both enquiry based and also contained concepts which pupils were expected to learn. MACOS was designed to reflect a coherent philosophy in which ideas were translated into terms that 'any learner' could master, with 'symbolic' knowledge represented in 'enactive' (action based) and 'eikonic' (visual) forms. Bruner's 'spiral curriculum' meant that pupils met increasingly complex examples of social behaviour and the major concepts of the course – life cycle, innate and learned behaviour, adaptation, natural selection, structure and function, information and communication – became increasingly meaningful for understanding the social behaviour being studied. (For the psychological underpinnings of Bruner's ideas, see *Understanding Classroom Learning,* Entwistle, 1987.)

MACOS, however, is hardly taught today. Its insistence on fidelity of implementation restricted dissemination to the enthusiasts who could find sponsorship to attend the training workshops. The problems of delivery in schools were formidable: the course's lesson outlines lasting 120 days threatened to take over the curriculum and the technical resources required to handle sixteen films, five filmstrips, four LP records, three simulation games and twenty-six booklets of materials were beyond what teachers singly could cope with or school management were prepared to support.

Another example of flawed curriculum development is Nuffield Combined Science (NCS), introduced in the sixties. Michael Shayer and Philip Adey (1981) demonstrated how the curriculum was too difficult for the typical pupil following it. This reflected piloting on an unrepresentative sample. Each unit, on which the course was structured, included activities beyond the intellectual reach of most pupils. Worse still, these activities were the key to understanding each unit.

These examples serve to highlight the fact that planning which does not take account of all the principles outlined above can be ineffective in the sense that products will not be adopted by teachers, or the developed curricula will damage pupils' self-concepts and put them off subjects they could well succeed in. How adequate, then, are current conceptions of planning at course level, and in terms of the wider national frameworks which have been developed in recent years?

Planning for successful learning

A course often comprises a number of 'subjects' or 'components' taken concurrently by a pupil. A subject can be thought of as a series of topics. The curriculum planner will wish to ensure that key ideas or skills in each topic are 'mastered' by the pupil, in the sense that he can give an account of their meaning or pass a given test on them. Mastery learning is associated with the names of Americans such as Robert Mager, James Block and Ben Bloom; some interesting applications of the idea to secondary subject teaching in a UK context have been reported by Harry Black and Bryan Dockrell (1980).

In the traditional programme each topic is considered as content to be covered by the teacher. Each topic is organised in relation to the other topics in terms of a sequence believed to be optimum for the pupil. There are several possible bases for sequencing (proceeding from the simple to the complex, or from the familiar to the unfamiliar are examples), and the teacher adopts one, goes through the materials and sets a test of attainment at the end

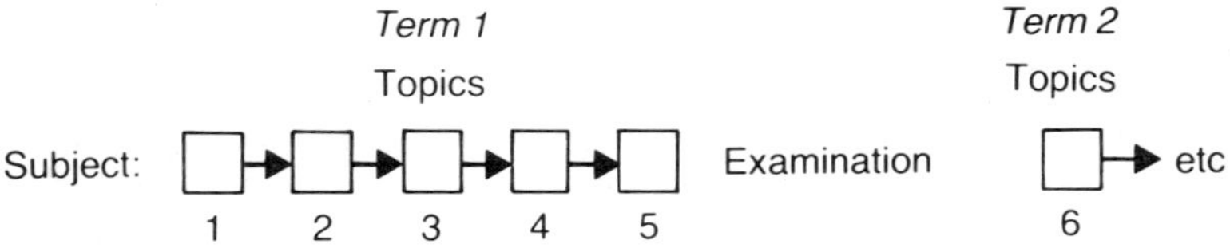

Figure 4.1. Conventional Teaching Structure

of the sequence (for example, the end of term). The structure for the subject (Term 1) is, therefore, as shown in Figure 4.1.

This model takes no account of pupil difficulties with the topics: a pupil who fails the examination has no opportunity for further learning of these topics, but carries his 'failure' into the next term and the new topics. If Term 2 topics are planned on the assumption that the pupil has mastered the material in Term 1 then clearly the pupil is going to encounter difficulties. If this pattern is repeated year by year, the pupil will be increasingly disadvantaged and demotivated.

An alternative 'mastery learning' approach involves conscious selection of key ideas within the topics to be studied. Sequencing

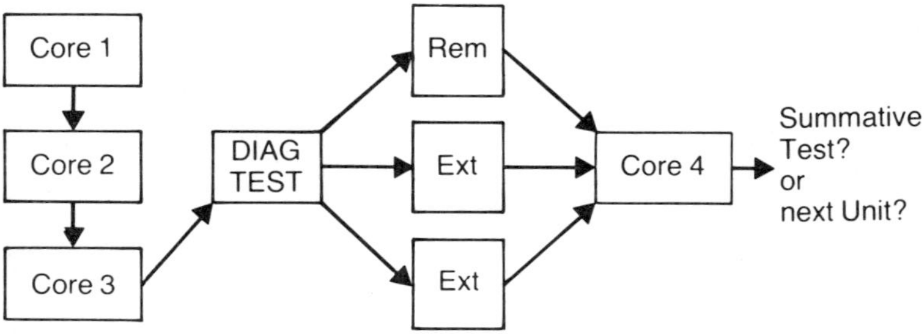

Core – Irreducible minimum for understanding and progression.

→ – Sequence of learning (note paths tend to diverge after the diagnostic test).

DIAG TEST – Diagnostic test, designed to pinpoint individual strengths and weaknesses (and hopefully to evaluate teaching methods or materials).

Rem – Work for remediation or reinforcement.

Ext – Work for extension or enrichment.

Figure 4.2 Simple Model Showing the Inter-relationship of Diagnostic Assessment and Teaching in any one Curricular Unit these carefully, and placing assessment at a point two-thirds of the way through the unit will provide evidence on the extent to which ideas have been grasped, and allow opportunity for remedial action, consolidation, and enrichment within the time available for the course depending upon the success of the pupil. By this means all pupils are offered maximum opportunity to master the basic skills the subject is concerned to develop. This pattern leads to the sequence set out in Figure 4.2.

Black and Dockrell found that up to seventy-five per cent of pupils in conventional teachings might fail to understand one or more of the key concepts covered in the core. Reasons differed, but in general high attainers might have been absent on the day the material was taught, while low attainers just had not grasped it, although they might have been successful on some of the other concepts. Under mastery learning conditions, all pupils have time for remediation to take place, and the most successful are able to extend their understanding through the variety of extension exercises which are provided. One outcome of this approach is the high level of cooperation fostered between teacher and pupil, and the confidence with which all pupils enter the next sequence.

Mastery learning on this model is clearly worthwhile and feasible provided the necessary hard work is put in during the planning stages. Black and Dockrell developed a collaborative research style with some dedicated teachers, working mainly with curricula in home economics, technical education, modern languages and geography for pupils in the first year of secondary school. The main problems they encountered were in helping teachers clarify the irreducible minimum of core material and key concepts they wished their pupils to learn, and in constructing diagnostic tests.

Identification of key concepts is a matter of subject expertise on the teacher's part in relation to the objectives being pursued. In another highly regarded Scottish study Mary Simpson and Brian Arnold (1983) explored the difficulties pupils encountered at O grade biology with some basic concepts such as osmosis and photosynthesis. Their content analysis of the ideas which, combined, gave meaning to these concepts highlighted the 'alternative frameworks' which pupils brought to learning new ideas. Thus the concept of 'food', which is basic to understanding photosynthesis, presented difficulties for pupils who interpreted it, in terms of their own experience, as something that you take into the body rather than as something which the organism makes for itself. Their point was that the subject expert who really understands the concept – and they found that even some teachers shared some of their pupils' misunderstandings – will be more sensitive to possible sources of confusion. Black and Dockrell make a similar point in their discussion of the principles on which diagnostic tests should be constructed: distractors in multiple choice items should be formed from common misconceptions which in some cases reflect naive commonsense conceptualisations or 'alternative frameworks' (see *Understanding Classroom Learning,* Entwistle, 1987).

Sequencing learning experiences on a mastery learning model can imply individualised learning through workcards and learning packages as is practised by many primary school teachers. In such a system pupils can present themselves for diagnostic testing when they feel ready, normally after completing the prescribed activities and self-assessing their own learning.

To summarise, the requirements for developing mastery learning are:

- analysing the conventional content into key skills and concepts necessary for attaining the performance criteria, and discarding what is peripheral;
- putting these into an appropriate sequence covering two-thirds of the available learning time;
- developing learning resources to help pupils acquire these skills/concepts;
- developing valid diagnostic tests of 'mastery' of the key skills and concepts;
- developing remedial exercises based on the likely misconceptions which have to be tackled, and extension units which will 'stretch' those who have coped successfully so far.

A team approach to design and try-out is necessary, and a commitment to developing the first draft into a better second draft. But the results obtained throw up all sorts of challenging questions about the appropriateness of the content, the meaning of 'mastery', responsibility for learning (teacher, pupil or both?), and the meaning of 'difficulty' of a course. Planning of this kind leads to the provision of quality learning experiences, but would also make heavy demands on resources of time and professional skill if it were to be advocated as the norm.

Quality of national frameworks

A series of DES reports since the 'Great Debate' has argued the case for a balanced curriculum for primary and early secondary education. (See also *The Core Curriculum,* Kirk, 1986.) The curriculum should be based on a common core of learning experiences, and should be relevant to life after school. GCSE relates to the 14–16 curriculum, and prescribes a subject-based course over two years, leading to three overlapping attainment levels in which performance is tied to grade-related criteria. In Scotland an equivalent examination (Standard Grade) was introduced in 1984 in some subjects. Another Scottish development, this time in relation to non-advanced further education at 16+, has seen the introduction of a modular National Certificate. Over 2,000 modules have been developed in a crash programme. Each module must conform to a set of criteria as regards length, level of attainment, teaching/learning approaches, and must be assessed on a criterion-referencing 'mastery' model at a single level of attainment. It is envisaged that these modules will link with work-based experiences to certificate the skills required in a wide variety of occupations.

In higher education the Council for Accreditation of Teacher Education (CATE) has spelled out criteria which teacher training institutions in England and Wales must meet for their courses to be approved, while CNAA has articulated stringent criteria of course planning.

The quality of frameworks reflects the process by which they were developed, and the understanding of issues of curriculum design and implementation. Maurice Holt (1983) criticises the DES publication *The School Curriculum* (DES, 1981) because, despite its claim to offer 'a national consensus on a desirable framework for the curriculum', it reflects the tone of an 'in-house' document rather than the outcome of widespread discussion with the range of interested parties. Consequently it lacks 'the clarity and understanding which can only come from discussion with those who have direct knowledge of the issues and problems', viz, teachers and academics (p. 40).

In Scotland comparisons have been made between the complexity of Standard Grade *vis- à- vis* the National Certificate. Elsewhere (Wilson, 1987) I have pointed out the comparison with GCSE. The flaws in the framework for Standard Grade include:

- the length of unit: subject courses over two years are a 'long' planning unit;
- the identification of content: courses have to be designed to reflect a number of 'elements' which are the essential skills of the course (elements in English include reading, writing, speaking and listening). Boundaries between elements are often hard to draw;
- levels of attainment: courses can lead to awards at three progressively differentiated levels, depending upon the nature of the subject matter studied, and success within it;
- assessment via grade-related criteria which attempt to define seven standards of performance in terms both of what pupils 'know, understand and can do', and also in relation to what other pupils are capable of.

Developing course proposals within the framework has proved daunting for teachers. So much so that in 1986 the SED issued a document which proposed that the number of elements to be considered in each subject be reduced, and directed teachers' attention to the main features which should differentiate children's work at different levels. The unrealistic demands of Standard Grade undoubtedly contributed to teacher militancy in Scotland, and has highlighted the question of the balance between central and locally based curriculum development.

The National Certificate also presents a challenge to further education, but it has advantages over Standard Grade in terms of its simplicity of structure, single level of attainment (students pass the module if they meet all the criteria which are the objectives of the course), and criterion-referenced assessment. Staff are required to define their objectives more precisely, to develop and justify the range of teaching and learning strategies employed, and to demonstrate that their assessment is indicating the students' level of competence in the required areas. One of the merits of modules is that, being single level, the issue of 'parity of esteem' is avoided: each module fulfils its own function and students take it because it is a means to the end they are pursuing.

Quality in national frameworks is important because these constitute challenges to schools and colleges to develop curriculum proposals and the programmes through which they will be implemented. Frameworks which neglect important design principles can be misleading while unrealistic demands can demoralise school management and the teaching profession. Frameworks which are well conceived can heighten levels of awareness of the issues in curriculum planning, and are more likely to stimulate a creative response from the school. In Britain there has been a movement towards school-based curriculum development over the past decade, and this will be discussed next.

Curriculum planning at the school level

Schools are organisations whose main task is to *deliver* a curriculum to pupils. Whatever development is attempted is against a background of 'business as usual', in that pupils must be taught, examinations must be prepared for, and the various activities of pastoral care attended to. Moreover their conditions of service are such that much of teachers' time in school is spent in face-to-face contact with pupils, and their free time is invariably occupied with correction or preparation for the next meeting with their class.

Studies of teachers in different countries indicate that they claim to spend between eleven hours (primary) and thirteen hours (secondary) per week in preparation and assessment. Preparation includes getting ready for class, and keeping abreast of developments in the curriculum; assessment includes marking, keeping records and invigilating. In terms of planning the actual process of class management, the most complex planning situation faces teachers of mixed ability classes who are expected to teach through groups and to offer pupils a 'differentiated' curriculum where tasks are matched to the capabilities of individual pupils.

The evidence from several studies is that group teaching and differentiation are rarely planned for. In primary, group work is often used by teachers mainly as an organisational device with pupils working individually on tasks, and group interactions playing little part in their completion. Kerry (1984) has shown that most teachers working with mixed ability secondary classes teach the class as one, pitching their lessons at a level just below that of pupils of average ability. Such grouping is often on the basis of perceived ability or pupil choice, but in the great majority of cases the content of the curriculum offered is the same, the only concession to 'slower' pupils being that the language of worksheets may have been simplified. In only a few cases is individualisation seriously attempted through the preparation of workcards and other resources, with the needs of slow learners being considered more fully than those of 'high flyers'.

To cope effectively with mixed ability classes, teachers need to devote more time to preparation and to be in schools with a wide range of accessible resources, particularly of the textbook and audio-visual variety. Their classroom management strategies require them to be flexible, with a capacity to use a variety of teaching modes within a lesson, to use a range of audio-visual media, to encourage a variety of pupil activities to progress simultaneously, and to involve pupils in taking responsibility for their own learning and decision making. The question of teacher 'flexibility' in managing learning in mixed ability classrooms has implications for how teachers are selected. The planning demands are such that it would be absurd to expect teachers to devise all the materials they need for teaching.

What role can and should teachers play in planning the development of the curriculum? Obviously, they have an important role in identifying the inadequacies of the existing curriculum. They can contribute ideas through membership of national curriculum teams, and be involved in the formative evaluation of new curriculum materials. In addition, many centrally resourced projects have moved away from conceptions of producing a 'teacher-proof' curriculum and instead have produced a few worked out exemplars and 'bonus' suggestions leaving it to teachers to adapt them for their own purposes. Teachers often need considerable help with this. In Scotland, such help may come, for example, from learning support teachers (the former remedial teachers) whose role is to assist class teachers to simplify and extend teaching materials (for example, worksheets) so that they are accessible to the range of pupils in a class. Also, structures can be devised to extend the possibilities of choice of curricula open to teachers. Pinchas Tamir (1986) has outlined how teacher autonomy is fostered in the Israeli high school, and his suggestions may be more valuable than the current British emphasis on schools individually presenting their own response to government guidelines. Teachers and individual schools in Israel are free to follow their own chosen topics outside the prescribed syllabus for up to twenty-five per cent of the class time, and teachers in schools with a good track record in presenting for the national matriculation examination can, subject to certain conditions, make judgments of pupils which contribute fifty per cent of the final assessment. Tamir observes that teachers seem to be interested in increased autonomy so long as they are free to determine how much responsibility they are taking on. The system he describes provides this opportunity for 'guided freedom' where teachers have a choice within a framework accepted by all the parties involved – teachers, administrators, inspectors, curriculum developers and examination boards.

What, then, should school-based planning focus on? To a large extent the agenda has been defined by the statement of government expectations for headteachers identified in the last chapter. The main aspects include:

- planning the school programme as a whole; identifying the school's overall objectives, and the contribution of different aspects of a pupils' programme to these;
- defining the structure of the curriculum in terms of core and options, mixed ability and single sex grouping, timetabling;
- developing school policies on assessment, multiculturalism, information technology, discipline, pastoral care, links with parents, feeder primaries and post-school institutions;
- developing a team approach to planning and delivery of the curriculum which breaks down teacher and departmental isolation, ensures the planning, development and sharing of resources for differentiation, and the pursuit of cross-curricular objectives (for example, in relation to literacy, numeracy and multiculturalism) by all teachers;
- developing strategies for monitoring and self-evaluation which command the confidence of all staff, and which serve to raise awareness about the extent to which objectives are being

achieved, customers and clients are satisfied and aspects for improvement are highlighted.

Management's role includes creating a climate in which planning is recognised to be important, providing leadership in how to go about it, creating a range of leadership roles and ensuring that appropriate staff fill them, providing the requisite level of support to enable them to see the planning task through in the timescale, and ensuring that the process leads to visible and worthwhile results in terms of approval of courses by validating bodies, satisfactory reports from HMI and advisory services, and high staff morale. But the most important outcome undoubtedly is the provision of better learning experiences for pupils.

The planning process

Many of the published texts on curriculum planning are either theoretical analyses, reviews or principles of curriculum design, or case studies of how particular schools or teachers have gone about developing practice. Theoretical analyses such as that produced by Hirst (1974) have been helpful to planners of the national curriculum framework. Another writer who has contributed at this level is Denis Lawton but his *School Curriculum Planning* (1986) states that 'it is for the school to decide how to convert general guidelines into a set of school syllabuses'. Writers such as W. J. K. Davies (1978), A. Romiszowski (1981 and 1984) and Derek Rowntree (1982) clarify issues in curriculum design with special reference to individualising learning. Douglas Barnes (1982) suggests practical exercises which can develop staff skills with real-life planning tasks. Drawing on extensive secondary school experience Philip Waterhouse (1983) also offers many practical suggestions for planning group and individual work with the aid of resources. Maurice Holt's *Curriculum Workshop* (1983) includes case studies of whole-school planning of project work in primary schools, and of how secondary schools developed flexible timetables. A Canadian text (F.M. Connelly *et al.*, 1980) focuses on the individual teacher rather than the team situation. Case studies such as are described in John Nixon's *A Teacher's Guide to Action Research* (1981) and Malcolm Skilbeck's *Readings in School-Based Curriculum Development* (1984) provide accounts of how particular planning issues were tackled. But more studies need to be undertaken of how teachers, especially in primary, plan group work over a period of time, select, deploy and exploit resources, manage their own and their pupils' time, and teach pupils how to operate within the system they have devised.

Planning a school policy or putting together a school response to guidelines produced by an outside body is a creative process. Experience suggests that it is worth distinguishing between 'committee' planning and 'task force' planning. The former is almost exclusively a deliberate exercise: a representative group, including outsiders to the institution, theorises about how the course should be structured, and allocates writing tasks to different members, so that a logical proposal emerges which meets the external criteria. The proposal is then subjected to scrutiny by a validating body, and after a face-to-face meeting between validators and planning team, the proposal is accepted (subject to amendment) or rejected. Such a mechanism ensures that considerable thought goes into the planning, and the force of external validation is to promote internal cohesion, the burying of interdepartmental hatchets, and an appearance of unity and cooperation, which may not last into the delivery stage of course.

The weakness of the committee approach is its exclusively theoretical stance. An action-research perspective combines deliberation with the test against experience. Action-research implies trial and adaptation as a means to developing policies and proposals. It is, in fact, the basis of most of the best curriculum development. Standard Grade and GCSE, for example, are often justified as simply following the lead of the most successful teachers. My own teaching strengths derive from trying out somewhat tentative ideas, reflecting on the response obtained from students, and building up clearer statements of intent in the light of practical experience. What I am asserting, in other words, is that the best plans derive from experience: planning documents which reflect exclusively theoretical perspectives, which are divorced from a cycle of piloting, modification in the light of feedback, and subsequent development are unlikely to be soundly based. Certainly when it comes to 'fleshing out' for delivery they will be capable of multiple interpretations, and in the absence of their authors, the spirit of the original may well be lost.

The most sophisticated planning I have undertaken was to develop the selection programme (Wilson and Mitchell, 1987) for entering teacher training students which is outlined in Chapter 7. The plan, essentially a curriculum for selection, emerged from a small task force and was drafted and implemented within three months. The model of selection was sophisticated and involved extensive work to develop documentation for candidates and for assessors. The administrative structure was complex, yet the system worked successfully.

Tom Peters and Nancy Austin (1984) argue that the classic way to develop innovations – large committees, systematic analysis of every facet of a problem, the search for a 'perfect' solution over a twelve to eighteen month timetable – does not reflect how innovations are produced in the real world of industry and commerce by successful entrepreneurs. Rather, the characteristics of successful development involve creating a prototype (60–90 days), evaluating it (60–90 days), developing a 'better' version (60–90 days), trying it out with a 'lead' user (i.e. not just a typical user, but someone prepared to experiment for you and give constructive feedback) and learning from that person. In other words, in business, the most successful development comes from 'successive approximations', and by creating a 'learning organisation', a sub-system within the larger organisation which produces plans and models and tries them out under conditions of enormous time pressure. The quality of such products is invariably higher than that produced by conventional means. It is interesting to reflect that our selection programme was developed within the 90 day timescale.

How should schools plan for quality?

This section offers some practical suggestions for task force planning. Some of the suggestions could be adopted by an LEA as well as by headteachers. Basic considerations concern paying attention to the context in which the proposal is to be implemented, and involving customers and clients in the process of planning.

Set up rival groups to work on common problems

An LEA can identify leading subject departments in different secondary schools to take responsibility for developing a local curriculum plan, An element of competition can spur staff to greater efforts. In-house training can be offered through setting up simulation exercises like that described in Figure 4.3. Results can be presented to a forum of advisers, principal teachers and others and this can stimulate debate and thinking. Within a primary school, a headteacher can get lower primary and upper primary teachers to plan separately and compare results.

Figure 4.3 Example of a Planning Exercise

1 Identify some subject content you normally teach pupils at a particular stage. Select an aspect of that content (for example a unit you would teach in two to three hours of classroom contact) and describe it. (Alternatively, an aspect of the informal curriculum such as the school assembly might be offered for the exercise.)

2 Specify objectives for teaching that content. Say why you wish pupils to learn it and what skills, understandings and attitudes you wish them to develop through learning about it. Write down not more that FIVE objectives and the order in which you would try to achieve them.

3 How would you assess whether your teaching has been effective? Describe how you would assess whether each objective had been attained i.e. what evidence on pupil performance would you wish to collect, how would you do it, and how would you interpret it?

Note on usage

This exercise may be set to primary or secondary teachers, working in small groups of not more than four. The group setting is important. Approximately forty-five minutes is required for discussion of planning, and a further forty-five for reporting back. Many issues relating to objectives, modes of assessment and the relationship between teaching, learning and assessment emerge in the course of this assignment.

(I am indebted to Dr W. Bryan Dockrell for introducing this exercise to me.)

Recognise that planning involves research, try out and reporting on development attempts

Good planning means identifying people with drive and ability. Selection of membership of the planning group is therefore critical. Likely recruits are staff who have recent experience in curriculum development or who have taken appropriate MEd or Open University courses or developed CSE Mode 3.

The essential thing is to get started and produce a draft proposal for some parts of the course that are being developed. A specification or outline is the first step, but the quality of a proposal is reflected in the 'fleshing out', that being the development of materials actually to be used in the teaching. Fleshing out of an element in the course may involve minor adaptation of existing resources, or major development work, but it provides the opportunity for try-out (ideally by members of the group who have not developed it) and the obtaining of consumer reaction. There is no 'right' model of curriculum development. What is needed, is for experimentation with a variety of approaches depending on the particular problem being considered.

Learn about curriculum planning from others

The best way to learn is from personal experience. But, other people's experience can be valuable as well as one's own. Twinning of schools, involvement of a consultant, attachment to a project, attendance at a short *ad hoc* training course, search of literature can all help promote skill in planning.

Report your curriculum planning

One of the advantages claimed for the committee approach, is that it generates commitment to the plan which is defended before the validating body. This commitment is often superficial and in fact the process can be immoral where staff are blackmailed into supporting an institutional proposal which, in their hearts, they do not believe to be sound, perhaps because it is untested.

Commitment to a defensible plan is, however, desirable, and those who develop curricula should be able to feed their experience into meetings with school management and staff who have to deliver the courses. Curriculum planning involves providing background and support to all those involved: the quality of delivery will depend on each person in the face-to-face situation providing uniform interpretation of the plan and the requisite level of support for pupils. School-based in-service training conducted by curriculum planning teams would be relevant and stimulating, provided that the quality of the development work is itself high.

Conclusion

This chapter has clarified the meaning of planning, and suggested ways in which schools might approach curriculum planning. It is not being suggested that there is no place for a committee model of school development; rather it is arguing that task forces operating on an action-research model will produce both curriculum proposals and policy suggestions of higher quality than mere deliberation. The lesson of the curriculum development projects of the sixties is not to abandon an empirical approach but to make it better! National frameworks which are feasible (for example, the Scottish National Certificate) can provide a structure within which teachers can develop courses, drawing principally upon materials developed elsewhere, but it is through fleshing them out and seeing if they 'work' that an understanding of the problems of promoting learning will be enhanced. It has been argued that not every teacher has the inclination – even if time were available – to adopt an action research stance to development, so management has to provide the conditions under which those with the interest and the drive can undertake it, while ensuring a degree of curriculum freedom to all. At the end of the process of curriculum planning, a course has to be delivered to pupils and teachers have responsibility for that delivery.

5

Quality of Delivery

Delivery means putting a plan into effect. The pupil is put into a learning situation designed by the teacher to stimulate learning. Learning situations can take many different forms, from face-to-face teaching in the classroom to the completion of a 'distance-learning' assignment alone. This chapter examines the meaning of quality of delivery in schools and colleges by considering how plans are interpreted by teachers, and pedagogical and interpersonal factors which affect the teacher's capacity to put the plan into effect.

Delivering a plan

Essentially 'delivering' a plan means putting the 'fleshed out' version into operation to achieve the outcome (i.e. behavioural changes) in the pupil which the written statement of the curriculum 'promised'. But plans differ in the extent to which such changes are clearly specified. Of the curriculum frameworks reviewed in the last chapter, only that developed for Scotland's National Certificate (for non-advanced further education) couples objectives and performance outcomes closely; most plans reflect a looser coupling, and where planners subscribe to expressive objectives, as in the aesthetic curriculum, only the learning situations may be defined and not the outcome to be expected. Planning, therefore, can result in teachers being tightly controlled, in that the teacher becomes, in effect, a technician operating a 'teacher-proof' curriculum, or it can leave teachers considerable freedom as to how they go about the task of teaching. Most plans – however detailed and prescriptive they may appear – leave considerable scope for interpretation to the teacher, particularly in relation to such matters as the selection of exemplars, and the balance of treatment of topics where only some aspects can be dealt with in the available time. Indeed the essential teaching skills in education, such as the strategy to get to the heart of the meaning in a poem, can be supplied only by the teacher.

The manner in which a plan is delivered by the teacher will reflect a number of factors. First, is the teacher aware of the plan? Curriculum guidelines may fail to be implemented because teachers are never told what the guidelines are, or do not understand what they mean. Second, assuming awareness and understanding, is the plan feasible and are there sufficient resources (materials, advice, time) to deliver it? Third, how committed to the plan is the teacher? Commitment is likely to reflect the teacher's involvement in developing the plan. The 'not invented here' syndrome takes many forms from simply ignoring the plan to undermining it by expressing views to pupils to the effect that the stated objectives are simply not worth pursuing. Strong commitment is not necessarily reflected in 'fidelity' in the delivery of the plan, however. Teachers may justify departure from tasks assigned (and spelled out in course documentation) in terms of 'bending and flexing' to the perceived needs of the pupil; such teachers would argue that there are numerous ways of delivering the objectives of a course, especially when these are rather vaguely defined, and that theirs was a more responsive way for that particular group of pupils. Such departures can, of course, affect pupils' perceptions of the seriousness with which the course is to be taken. The extent to which a plan will be delivered with 'fidelity' will also depend upon the nature of the subject matter and the level of curriculum; fidelity being greater perhaps in maths and sciences, especially at school level, and less in more expressive areas. Fidelity between plan and delivery may be expected to be highest of all where the individual teacher has planned her work with the specific needs of her pupils in mind, and delivery means putting into effect her own plan. Experienced teachers delivering their own 'successful', courses may indeed express puzzlement that they should be expected to produce written plans when they teach 'intuitively' knowing what 'works' with pupils, and valuing the flexibility of modifying their strategy as particular issues emerge which preoccupy their students.

In most cases, therefore, planning does not solve the problem of delivery; its function, rather, is to clarify what teachers should be trying to achieve with pupils, and to identify the strategies to be employed (and the resources to be deployed) to do so. It remains for the teacher actually to deliver.

The teacher and delivery

For the teacher to be an effective deliverer of the curriculum she must understand what the pupil currently knows, have a capacity to devise appropriate learning situations in the light of that knowledge, and skill in managing them so their potential for promoting learning is realised. (Further relevant discussions can be found in *Understanding Classroom Learning,* Entwistle, 1987.)

Finding out what the pupil currently knows

Ben Bloom (1978) developed a model of learning to summarise his view of what was known about what affects success in school learning, shown in Figure 5.1.

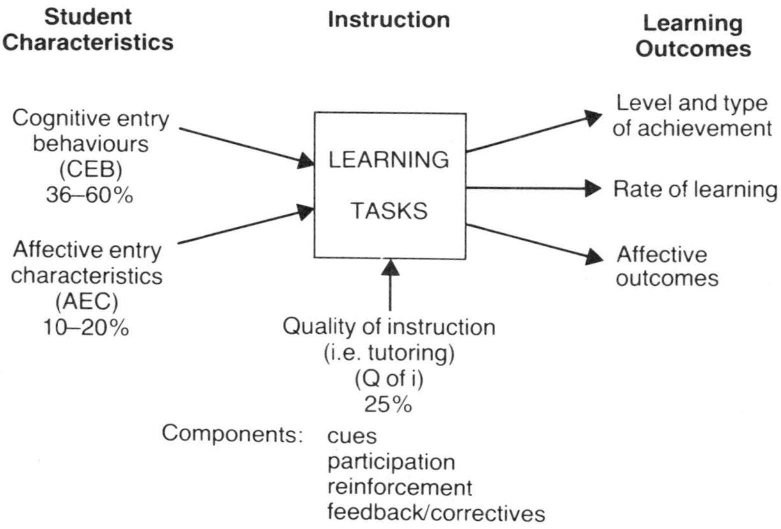

Figure 5.1. Bloom's Model of Factors Affecting Success in Learning

Bloom maintains that the two relevant sets of factors are cognitive entry behaviours (i.e. knowledge and skills relating to language, numeracy and the specific content to be learned), and affective entry characteristics (i.e. attitude to learning and confidence of success). Together he suggests that these account for between 46 and 80 per cent of the variation in achievement in the new learning task. Whatever credence one places on such estimates, it is reasonable to accept the important effect of past learning on the likelihood of success in new learning tasks.

Assessing pupils' skills and attitudes is more time-consuming for the teacher starting with a new group of pupils (a new class in primary or a class entering secondary) than where the teacher is working continuously with pupils and keeping records from day to day. Ideally, programmes should 'articulate' to each other in the sense that the 'infant' curriculum should link up closely with that in junior school, or school certificate courses with programmes in the first year of higher education, but again, with the exception of the National Certificate (where entry levels for modules are defined in terms of competences attained on earlier modules, or relevant work experience) this rarely happens. Bennett (1984) and his colleagues, for example, found that at infant-junior transfer receiving teachers often taught content that was already familiar to the pupils. Pupil record cards are rarely sufficiently detailed to be helpful to the receiving school or class teacher, although some of the new *Records of Achievement* (see Law, 1984) contain more helpful information. Many schools administer objective tests and some teachers have their own home-made diagnostic assessments to discover strengths and weaknesses. Writing tasks can be set to identify attitudes, expectations and fears, (for example, at age of transfer to secondary) and inventories have also been devised for this purpose. Where the aim is to raise students' consciousness of their own attitudes to learning and current study skills, awareness-raising exercises of the type described in *Improving Study Skills* (Selmes, 1986) or in *Teaching Students to Learn – A Student Centred Approach* (Gibbs, 1981) may be introduced. The fact is, however, that little systematic attempt is made to assess the knowledge, skills and attitudes of the entering pupil and even where that is done, to exploit the information consciously by designing courses which reflect the pupil's strengths and weaknesses.

In day-to-day classroom situations, teachers of course have a shrewd idea of what their pupils understand and can do. Since much teaching is incremental – building step-wise on ideas and operations already taught – assessing previous learning can often be undertaken in a short preliminary review.

Devising appropriate learning situations

Bloom's model also draws attention to the importance of 'quality of instruction' by the teacher in promoting learning. In Chapter 2 we reproduced his account of the model tennis coach. But modelling has to be of the relevant skills. David Berliner (1985) has observed that:

> 'The single most important factor in predicting whether or not a teacher will be effective is whether the curriculum that is delivered to students in his or her classroom is linked logically or empirically to the outcomes that are desired.' (p.128)

Curriculum delivery is both about what the teacher does, and, more significantly, what the teacher enables the pupils to do. The balance between these is important. But as Berliner emphasises, the learning experiences must be such as to enable the objectives to be realised.

With regard to direct instruction, where the teacher adopts an expository teaching mode to introduce a topic, or structure the subject matter, it is obviously of crucial importance that the teacher chooses content relevant to the objectives, knows what she is talking about, and can explain herself in a way which will be clearly understood by her pupils. Invariably this means translating 'difficult' ideas, perhaps by providing resource-based examples in the eikonic (visual) or enactive (doing) mode rather than the symbolic (words or numbers). For example, translating the difficult concept of 'symmetry' into readily understandable and amusing terms, as I once observed, where a teacher summoned a pupil to the front of the P5 class and posed the question as to whether a symmetrical division of Jim would be obtained by cutting him in half at the waist or down the middle! Factors such as the extent to which presentation is organised around a coherent, logically developed structure, contextualised in terms of previous learning experiences and pointing up implications for future activities, delivery is at a pace likely to sustain interest, rather than being too fast or too slow, and issues are presented as problems to be thought about or matters already resolved are all relevant to quality of direct instruction.

However, the quality of pupil learning experiences is increasingly perceived to reflect the teacher's ability to select and allocate appropriate tasks which 'match' the pupil's ability. The aim of good matching is to 'avoid the twin pitfalls of demanding too much and expecting too little'. The able child should be 'stretched', while the weakest should be set tasks on which they can experience success. The quality of different tasks, too, is worth considering in terms of the kinds of intellectual demands they make on children.

The evidence from studies by Bennett *et al*. (1984) in infant schools and Kerry (1984) in first-year secondary mixed-ability classes is that teachers experience considerable difficulty in matching. Bennett clarified the nature of tasks set in terms of the kinds of intellectual demands they placed upon pupils. He identified five different kinds as shown in Table 5.1, below:

Kind of Task	Chief Characteristics	Example
Incremental	Introduces new ideas, procedures or skills, demands recognitions, discriminations.	Having done sums with money the child is introduced to the idea of 'change'.
Restructuring	Demand a child invents or discovers an idea for himself.	The relationships between numbers.
Enrichment	Demands application of familiar skills to new problems.	Problem solving or projecting into an unknown situation.
Practice	Demands the tuning of new skills on familiar problems.	Tell a well-known story (for example, David and Goliath) in your own words.
Revision	Demands the use of skills which have not been practised for some time.	Revising number bonds.

NB It has to be borne in mind that these are simply ways of describing tasks: there is no intrinsic reason for any type of task to be seen as superior or inferior to others. But different kinds of tasks make qualitatively different intellectual demands on learners.

Table 5.1 The Nature of Tasks in Language and Maths set by Infant Teachers

Source: Bennett *et al.* (1984) *The Quality of Pupil Learning Experiences:* Lawrence Erlbaum Associates

What Bennett found, however, was the predominance of practice tasks, particularly in the language curriculum, the very similar pattern of task demands set by teachers for children at different levels of attainment, and the gap between the task demands the teachers thought they were making on their pupils (especially the high attainers) and those they were actually making. Teachers very rarely saw a task as too easy for a child, wasteful of a child's time, beneath his attainment level or not challenging. On the other hand they perceived almost one in three of the number tasks they set, and one in four of the language tasks, as presenting difficulties for their pupils.

Quality of matching a task to a pupil reflected two factors: the teacher's skill in diagnosing a pupil's learning difficulties, and capacity to design tasks which actually made the demands claimed. Mismatches in task demand occurred often because the teacher did not ascertain that the child was already perfectly familiar with the task content, so that incremental tasks in fact became practice tasks. The discrepancy between actual and intended task demands can be illustrated from a lesson where a teacher wanted to improve her pupils' grasp of sentence structure. Having used a picture to form a basis for class discussion and having drawn attention to key features, such as capital letters and full stops, the teacher then set a 'missing word' exercise which required a knowledge of the meaning of words, but did not require attention to the structure of sentences in the sense used by the teacher

Another gap observed by the study related to quality of differentiation of the pupil experience, that is the extent to which the teacher individualises the pupil's programme and exploits the potential of group learning. In most primary classes it is normal for pupils to be grouped for reading and number, and to undertake work prescribed on workcards or otherwise set by the teacher. There is little doubt that, in many classes, grouping enables children to cover different content, and to proceed at a faster rate than they would in a whole-class teaching situation. Even so, there are considerable differences in curricular coverage between classes where pupils are grouped in similar ways. Bennett confirmed earlier findings that most of the talk in groups was not related to the task, that conversations were not sustained and that boys tended to talk only to boys and girls to girls. Teacher-pupil interactions in number work were largely procedural, with the teacher rarely diagnosing where a child's strategy was at fault. Much of their time was absorbed in correcting the sums they had set (most at practice level) as pupils queued for attention. In language, the teacher's instructional input was mainly in providing or correcting spelling. Teachers were preoccupied with form (number of sums correct, applying the conventions of language work) rather than with the *meaning* of the performances, or with the quality of what was being learned.

Kerry dichotomised classroom tasks as 'low level' and 'high level'. Low level tasks included copying or writing headings, memorising and reading aloud. High level tasks made imaginative demands, required the collection of evidence, problem solving, analysis and synthesis. He concluded that task setting occurred frequently in most classes (an average of 4.3 tasks per eighty-minute double lesson), that the vast majority (more than eighty per cent) of tasks set were low level, and that subject areas such as integrated studies, English and science, made greater cognitive demands than RE and geography. Kerry concluded that:

> 'Most task setting provides undifferentiated work for pupils who differ widely in ability; that such task setting contradicts the underlying philosophy of individual growth in mixed-ability classes; that few tasks make adequate cognitive demands on the able, in many cases not even on the average pupils, and that much time is spent on tasks which are simply trivial.' (pp. 177–8)

To improve the quality of matching means increasing teachers' capacity for self-evaluation, and developing their skills of task setting, diagnosis and remediation. Bennett emphasises that teachers need to listen to children's explanations of why they have tackled set tasks in particular ways, and from that to deduce the nature of their miscomprehension. But this demands considerable expertise in the nature of the subject matter to be learned. In mathematics, for example, many primary teachers appear not to have that level of understanding themselves, and so are not capable of explaining a particular rule in any way other than they themselves learned it. Skill of translating an idea into terms that a child can understand depends, in short, both upon the knowledge base of the teacher and the pedagogical skills through which she can communicate that insight to the child. But quality of delivery also extends to skill in managing the children, and in establishing and maintaining good personal relationships with pupils.

Managing the learning process

Several aspects of teacher behaviour have been related to the management of learning. In the USA the Beginning Teacher Evaluation Study (BTES) found differences in the relationship between student achievement and a teacher's ability to keep students attending on tasks, or 'engaged'. The study found that the percentage of engaged time in five grade 5 (age 11+) maths classes ranged from fifty to ninety per cent. Studies of individual pupils have shown that some are adept at avoiding any work at all in the course of a morning. Berliner (1985) identified the following factors as relevant to effective teaching: monitoring, structuring, pacing, questioning, climate factors, use of tests and grades and feedback. He summed up their influence as follows:

> 'Monitoring keeps engagement high, thus influencing achievement. Structuring helps students know what is expected, thus influencing success with the tasks they work at. Pacing, when rapid, ensures that a maximum amount of the curriculum to be learned is provided to the student. Thus, it affects opportunity to learn. Questioning influences attending in classrooms and reveals something about the content of the tests if the questions are related to the desired outcomes and not just time fillers. This is true of questions at any cognitive level. Wait-time after questioning

> seems to influence attending by requiring deeper processing than is ordinarily the case, and by influencing success rate, apparently by insuring that enough time is granted to correctly answer thoughtful questions. The climate variables, such as communicating academic expectations, apparently influences motivation, positively or negatively, thereby affecting the engaged time students put into acquiring skills and information. A safe and orderly classroom, where there is evidence of academic focus, also allows for higher rates of engaged time in the academic tasks, presumably those related to academic outcomes. The sensible management of deviancy keeps interruptions to a minimum, insuring high levels of engagement. A convivial atmosphere develops the trust and cooperation necessary to complete academic tasks successfully. Tests and grades used as summative information for students are motivating and increase total engaged time in academic pursuits. When used as formative information, tests and grades also reveal something of the nature of the outcome measure. They also help to ensure higher rates of success by the nature of the feedback they provide learners. Feedback such as praise or using student ideas increases motivation, thereby ensuring higher rates of engagement. Corrective feedback affects error rate, ensuring higher levels of success experience.' (p. 150)

In Britain Robert Laslett and Colin Smith (1984) have suggested rules of classroom management which will enable teachers to establish and maintain a peaceful work-oriented classroom atmosphere, and to avoid confrontations. Effective management depends not only on skilful handling of entry to, and exit from the classroom, but also in presenting tasks of variety and challenge, varying the pace and making smooth transitions between activities, with the teacher keeping the initiative in knowing her pupils, their characteristics and foibles, with monitoring of behaviour, marking their efforts in a positive and constructive spirit and being mobile within the classroom, so that she can be close to all pupils over time and in particular to those who are likely to be disruptive. Quality teachers do their best to limit confrontation with individual pupils through avoiding public denigration or sarcastic comments, through selective deafness to remarks which are unattributed, through using non-verbal communication, particularly physical proximity to the disruptive pupil, eye contact, or frowns where these are likely to be effective, through avoiding physical intervention which can escalate in unpredictable ways, and through apologising when that is appropriate.

While all teachers find difficulty in establishing and maintaining good personal relationships with some pupils, some have acute problems with many of the classes they teach. Laslett and Smith (1984) classify teachers as 'imperturbables', 'resilients;, and 'irritators', and provide pen portraits of each. The effectiveness of one 'imperturbable' maths teacher was held to lie in his respect for the children. This showed in the way he spoke to them (never shouting), listened to them, in the work he set (which was demanding) and in the care which he marked and went over homework. A second aspect of his effectiveness was the thoroughness with which he prepared his lessons, and his knowledge of the pupils. A third was his demeanour in the classroom, with low voice and quiet movement around the class, and his organisation of his classroom environment. Finally his meticulous record-keeping ensured that pupils worked to avoid having any 'black marks' entered against them in his notebook, since that could lead to detention and extra work. The effectiveness of a 'resilient' craft teacher lay in the way she insulated children who did not work or were noisy from others in the class, and the graduated way in which she dealt with pupils who did not conform, pointing to the consequences of not cooperating. She refused to get into a confrontation with a pupil, prefering to refer such children to a senior colleague, although she was always willing to talk with the disruptive child privately, thus demonstrating her respect for him.

While both the above teachers demonstrated skill in 'insulating deviancy' a geography teacher exhibited characteristics reminiscent of what has been labelled as 'deviance-provocative' behaviour (see Hargreaves *et al.*, 1975). Such teachers act on a number of assumptions about pupil motives which exacerbate conflict. For example they:

- assume that children whom they define as deviant do not wish to work, and will avoid it whenever possible;

- believe that it is not reasonable for them to provide conditions under which the children will work, if these are different from the conditions under which other children work successfully;
- believe that discipline is a contest between teachers and children that the teacher must win;
- believe in the value of confrontations and becoming involved in them;
- consider children as being anti-authority and anti-school rules;
- neglect deviant children in interactions in the classroom;
- expect children to behave badly;
- believe that children, on the whole, are not to be trusted, and deviant children certainly are not.

Their actions reflect these assumptions. Thus they:

- frequently issue ultimatums;
- punish inconsistently;
- make frequent sarcastic references;
- are unable to defuse tense situations;
- avoid informal contacts with children outside the classroom;
- make many negative evaluations on deviant children – to them and to colleagues.

Isca Salzberger-Wittenberg *et al.*, (1983) have drawn attention to how teachers' attitudes to pupils are shaped by their own childhood desires, wishes, fears, hate and love, the picture of adulthood which they have taken into their mind, and their assumptions about the adult-child relationship. Teachers see themselves in a variety of roles in relation to pupils, sometimes as a passer-on of knowledge and skills, as agents of their success, as a means to their personal development, and – especially with adolescents – as friends. But they are also afraid of criticism, of hostility and of losing control. An increasing number of teachers complain of stress, and the anxiety which this may reflect will be communicated to pupils in the way they manage lessons and their personal interaction with them. While predisposition to stress and neuroses is something which should be considered in selecting candidates for teacher training, the school organisation is the means for offering assistance to teachers who are coping with the problem. Berliner (1985) comments:

> 'It would appear easier to be an effective teacher if one is in an effective school, one that promotes safety, order, a business–like atmosphere, and seems to hold high expectations for achievement and finds ways to reward such achievement.' (pp. 133–4)

The maintaining of relationships depends on pupils as well as the teacher. Most pupils experience only minor problems in school but there is a proportion of children in trouble, who manifest a range of problems from personal inadequacy to anti-social traits. Some express a *cri de coeur* for understanding and emotional support because their parents do not understand them, or their family has disintegrated; others develop a 'crush' which the teacher may find difficult in coming to terms with, others again may be aloof, independent, insulting and violent. All teachers experience some degree of stress in coping with such students, especially when they themselves are physically exhausted or when morale is low.

Conclusion

In Chapter 2 it was stated that quality of the individual teacher's performance can be understood in terms of 'match' and 'personal capacity'. Match referred to the relationship between the demands and expectations made of teachers by their employers (for example the resources provided for the task to be undertaken). Poor match in this sense can put the teacher in an impossible situation so far as delivery is concerned. This chapter has discussed quality of delivery in terms of the teacher's *personal capacity,* that is, the skill with which the teacher plays the 'good teacher' role, in a situation where she is formally qualified to undertake the teaching and adequately resourced.

Questions have been explored about the relationship between a plan and its delivery. The essential feature of a good plan is that it clarifies for teachers the kinds of development in the pupil that are to be sought. Planning guidelines may indicate the general nature of the learning experiences which will bring these developments about; 'fleshing out' by those who are to deliver it will take the process further for specific pupils in a defined context, but realisation still depends upon how the teacher handles the face-to-face situation. Plans will be realised with different degrees of fidelity depending upon the teacher's understanding of the plan, her level of commitment to it, and her personal capacity to create and manage learning situations to realise its objectives.

Quality of delivery means providing learning experiences that deliver the objectives of the plan. Such learning experiences will be effective only in so far as they take into account what pupils already know and structure what has to be learned in imaginative ways which are both authentic to the subject matter, through which skills are to be developed, and match the interests and current levels of understanding of pupils. In addition the teacher has to provide variety, consolidate what is already known, challenge the imagination and set the pupil attainable targets. Quality of delivery also means effectively managing children as well as the learning process so that pupils are committed to working with the teacher towards a worthwhile end.

The ultimate test of quality of delivery must be in terms of the activities individual pupils are allowed or required to engage in by the teacher, the justification of these in terms of the objectives being pursued, and the achievements to which they can lead.

6

Evaluating and Improving the Quality of Teacher Performance

It has been argued in this book that quality in teaching involves providing the optimum curriculum for the individual pupil. The evidence as to whether this goal is being achieved is to be found in the work that children produce and the mental qualities and attitudes they manifest. Of course, as has been indicated earlier, the teacher is not solely responsible for the achievements or non-achievements of pupils, especially if through mismanagement she is given an impossible role. But in most circumstances the teacher is acknowledged to be the single most influential factor in the pupil's learning. In this chapter we consider what is meant by quality in learning, aspects of teaching where evidence can be collected which could improve performance, the problems and means by which, at school level, teachers can be helped to improve their practice, and how institutional performance as a whole can be developed.

Pupils' work as evidence of quality in learning

Filling up children's time at school with routine undemanding tasks is not unusual. Children will comply willingly. A classroom where pupils are 'engaged' in activities may therefore convey a misleading impression that 'quality learning' is occurring. It is not so much 'involvement' in the work that is a sign of 'quality learning', as the achievements of the children.

Hugh Hawes and William Holderness (1984) have pointed to hard criteria on quality in the work produced by children. Although written for supervisors and evaluators in African primary schools their suggestions are equally relevant in the British context. Children's work can tell us about what children are achieving, what aspects of the curriculum are being covered, and to what standard by the teacher and about the learning difficulties individual children are experiencing.

Children's work takes different forms, and serves different purposes, and can be found in exercise books, tests and examinations, individual contributions to project work, art work, and collections of materials. Work is set to promote the development of knowledge and skills, to encourage problem-solving and the development of ways of rational thinking, to stimulate creative thinking, and to foster the development of positive attitudes in working with others or in the local community. A quality programme will seek to balance these different purposes. But children's work can also indicate a great deal about many aspects of teacher performance including how the teacher manages the resources available to her, how she prepares, how she relates to pupils, especially with regard to individual differences, and how she assesses their progress. With regard to resources, for example, does she ensure that all children have access to the available resources? In African schools with poor facilities this might mean ensuring that each child has an exercise book, while in a school in Britain it might refer to the distribution of opportunities to work with the microcomputer.

Quality of preparation can be gauged by checking to see whether the information given by the teacher (including her spelling) is correct, and whether important ideas and skills have been highlighted rather than trivia. The selections a teacher makes from the official or prescribed syllabus can indicate whether she has a rationale for the curriculum that is taught. The nature of the programme followed by the teacher can emerge from considering how far the work undertaken is likely to relate to the interests of the children, whether open-ended as well as closed exercises have been set, what audiences pupils have been encouraged to write for (always the teacher, or to peers, or a public audience?), the level of difficulty in the work set (for example, full of mistakes, unfinished, or too easy and repetitive), and the degree to which work is graded and children show evidence of progressing. The extent to which special appropriate work is set for children with learning difficulties is another factor in quality.

The quality of assessment refers to the nature of the assessment tasks she sets, the feedback she provides pupils on their work and the records she keeps. An obvious point is the extent to which tests set actually relate to the programme which children have been studying in terms of checking that key ideas and skills have been mastered. Equally, however, the soundness of marking and the nature of the feedback provided to pupils are also important, with the use of appropriate marking techniques to convey maximum information for minimum time and effort, and with feedback being used to help children develop and progress in their work (for example, through encouraging revisions to first drafts of written work).

The keeping of adequate records is another factor in quality. Records can include impressionistic as well as numerical data, but are valuable insofar as they serve to inform teachers' actions and to provide children and parents with a mirror on progress, and potential. A visitor to the classroom, too, can get an impression of vitality of a class from the work on display, evaluating it in terms of its recency, topicality, usefulness for learning and teaching (for example, is it well-labelled and does it provoke questions?), and for motivating pupils.

A more effective, if more time-consuming, way of gauging the quality of pupil understanding is through listening to how pupils themselves explain the reasoning behind the work they do and the answers they offer. Studies by Peel (1960) with pre-adolescents, by Simpson and Arnold (1983) with adolescents learning biology, and by Marton, Pask and others with students in higher education (see Wilson, 1981) have obtained similar findings. Articulation requires the learner to declare his current level of understanding. As a result important clues are provided to the teacher as to the misconceptions that have been formed, and the way in which the task demands are perceived and acted upon. The skilled and sensitive teacher can then see what kinds of interventions by him are required to assist the learner. For this to happen, however, the teacher must first be willing to listen, and subsequently to possess the diagnostic skills to explore the basis of the learner's current understanding. Many teachers do not appreciate the significance of listening, lack the relevant diagnostic skills, and have no framework through which to interpret the evidence the learner provides. Bennett *et al.* (1984) for example, found that teachers in infant departments seldom tried to understand why children made errors in their number work; the teachers assumed the pupils had misunderstood, or had not been paying attention, and repeated their original explanations rather than exploring the answers with the children themselves.

At the heart of the curriculum is a concern for meaning. Children answer in ways that are meaningful to them; quality teaching involves understanding the basis of these meanings and trying to enrich them. Teachers need to be trained to be sensitive to the different frameworks of meaning within which different learners may operate; they also need help to develop the skills and attitudes which will enable them to explore these successfully.

Self-evaluation as the means to improving quality

The quality of work achieved by pupils is likely to be improved if the teacher comes to recognise that she is largely responsible for it, and if she is offered assistance to secure better results. This implies putting an emphasis on teacher self-evaluation as the first step to improving teaching quality, but doing so in a supportive and non-threatening context. Considerable evidence suggests that the factors which most motivate teachers to develop their practice include their own knowledge of, and interest in, what they are teaching, their skill as teachers and sense of professionalism, and their desire to provide their pupils with stimulating learning experiences.

In a number of countries a tradition of teacher self-evaluation has developed and collaborative networks of classroom teachers, teacher educators and educational researchers have been established. In UK the Classroom Action Research Network (CARN) was established at Cambridge Institute of Education in 1976. The Network grew from the work of Lawrence Stenhouse in the Humanities Project and the Ford Teaching Project directed by John Elliott and was stimulated by the materials produced by the Open University (1981). Its basic idea involves teachers opening up their practice to observation by others, or studying their own classroom practice to understand better the basis for their actions, and the relationship between intentions and achievements. The technique of triangulation, for example, enables the teacher, pupils and an independent observer to offer their differing accounts of the same lesson. It allows the teacher to clarify her intentions, the pupils to state how they perceived the reality created by the teacher, and the observer to present his own account of the interaction in the classroom as he has observed it.

One key idea is using action-research as a basis of professional development is that teachers have a tremendous store of tacit or unrecognised professional knowledge which is the basis on which they act. This knowledge is acquired in the course of their work and is reflected in the way in which they 'know' how to handle a class, for example, or introduce a particular topic into the curriculum. Professional development involves making this tacit professional knowledge conscious by becoming clearer about the relationship between actions and their effects, so that there is greater congruence between them.

Margot Cameron-Jones' (1985) work with seventy-nine Scottish teachers led her to recommend the following steps that a classroom teacher might take to analyse and develop her practice:

Step 1	Choose a general idea and analyse it:	One that is educationally important; an issue, small enough to work on, on which you can have an impact realistically and with hope of success. For example, the different amounts of time spent individually with different pupils, and whether these differences are justifiable or should be changed/improved.
Step 2	Make a reconnaissance of your present teaching:	Choose a method which: you can use or learn to use; you judge to be appropriate to your work; gives you best value for time; is personally acceptable to you.

Step 3	Devise an *action plan*, i.e. hypothesis, viz:	'I will do X with a view to improving Y.' Be clear about your reasons for doing it; limit severely what you attempt; be specific about *what* you are going to do; choose precisely the situations in which you are going to take the action; decide clearly on the *time* you will spend on the action (keep to it); think of how you will handle the *effects* of doing what you are planning to do; specify exactly *what you will monitor* and the *methods* you will use.
Step 4	Take the action you have planned and	
Step 5	Monitor it, i.e. focus on:	The action you are taking; the situation in which you are taking it; the effects it seems to be having (on you and on your pupils).
Step 6	Reflect, i.e. consider whether you are:	Improving your teaching; deepening your understanding of it; considering how best to build on the process of improvement you have begun.

This project also produced materials and advice which would support the process of development. Methods of observation were suggested. These included making a mental running commentary of what was happening in the classroom, selective observation regarding aspects of practice (for example, praise/blame statements) which were of central concern, and noting down key words and phrases, making running notes, tallies or frequencies of particular kinds of behaviour (for example, 'on task', 'not on task'), shadow study, seating charts, tape-recording, and using a colleague as a 'critical friend'. Writing up recollections in the form of diaries, or anecdotal records, and making transcripts of tape-recordings were other possibilities.

Materials developed by the project were trialled with different groups of teachers. They proved useful for individual teachers, for staff groups over a period of development, and for 'one-off' staff meetings. But two issues surfaced – the time available to teachers to undertake analysis and development, and the capacity of professional staff to support and facilitate the process. With regard to time, the project suggested that given an appropriately supportive institutional ethos,'one hour per week given 1:1 as individual attention to the teacher by someone facilitating her development skilfully will fuel that development very considerably'.

The role of facilitator, however, was viewed as problematic. Headteachers, and school management in general, had little experience of working in the advocated one-to-one situation helping staff analyse and evaluate their practice. The project suggested the following four practical ways in which all heads could act as facilitators at the present time:

1 Create the climate for staff development: for example, establish the idea that it is professionally desirable to want to change, develop, improve, no matter how good the teacher may already be.

2 Provide practical support: by making time for teachers, securing resources (for example, video, rooms, tape-recorders), organising and running group meetings effectively.

3 Provide emotional support: by recognising intensity of work involved, the anxiety teachers feel about exposing their work to others, the need for encouragement and optimism.

4 Re-channel dead-ends: for example, help the teacher see what she has really found out about her teaching even if on first impression she believes she has learned 'nothing useful'. This may mean helping the teacher *reconstruct* the general idea she is working on and guide her to a more fruitful focus (for example, using a different observational methodology) for the next part of her study.

Such facilitation can certainly support the teacher, but the wider implication is that headteachers should be selected for their potential to play such developmental roles, and trained in the conceptual and professional skills which would enable them to promote skills of analysis, reflection and creative action in their staff. In short, we have here a further manifestation of the mismatch (referred to in Chapter 3) between the expectations held for promoted staff and their capacity to meet them.

Consultancy for development of teacher and school

An alternative to 'in-house' development from management in a school is to secure the services of a 'consultant', if one is available. Consultants may be staff in the school or in other schools with special expertise in assessment or curriculum development, or learning difficulties, or they may be members of other institutions such as advisory services, colleges of education, universities and independent agencies. Consultants can often play a useful evaluative role with the teacher or with school management in providing an audience for reflection on practice.

Nixon (1981) reports the categories of conversations a consultant history lecturer had with different teachers. They covered organisational matters (for example, timing of lessons), matters relating to lesson planning, resourcing and the fears of teachers, reviews of lessons that had been shared, specific conversations about long-term planning for teaching a topic over a number of weeks, implications of resource-based learning for a future history scheme, personal and domestic matters, how the project would develop after the departure of the consultant, etc. In terms of 'unfreezing' attitudes and opening up the possibilities of change, the consultant can have a powerful catalytic effect if he has the requisite skills, has the confidence of those he is working with, and does not raise unreal expectations. In higher education, Boud and McDonald (1981) have advocated setting down in a 'letter of understanding' between consultant and client what their respective roles are, what the scope of the project is, and how it is to be conducted. In Scotland, remedial teachers are being retrained for a role which involves acting as a consultant to the class teacher in differentiating the curriculum to make it accessible to pupils with with special educational needs, so that they have consultancy 'with powers', although in practice these have to be exercised cautiously if their work is to be effective.

Consultancy is the means adopted by Per Dalin and his colleagues (1983) to promote the goals of the Institutional Development Programme (IDP) for school improvement. This programme makes the school the unit of reform. It sees schools as systems which include five major elements as follows:

1 The environment: 'the persons and organisations external to any focal organisation with which it must transact in order to survive' (pp. 44–5). Schools exist in a context of central and local government, colleges of education, research and development agencies, parent groups, teacher associations, other schools and educational services such as child guidance. The wider social, political and economic context also informally influences school policy and practice.

2 Institutional values: 'the fundamental beliefs of the members of the institution, especially as they are exemplified through philosophies, rituals, ceremonies and symbols' p. 45). Formal aims and objectives for the school will be stated, but these may not always coincide with the objectives actually pursued, and individual staff may endorse the official goals with varying degrees of enthusiasm.

3 Organisational structure: the structure as it might appear in an organisational chart. 'It includes decision-making structure, task structure and communications structure. It also consists of the institution role and classroom role which exist, the type and flow of the task and time structures, the physical context and material resources available, and the regulations which are reflected in policies, rules and formal guidelines' (p. 45).

4 Human relations 'the interpersonal aspects of an organisation as manifested in the communications system, the internal influence and power structure, the behavioural norms as reflected especially in meetings, as well as the general climate of the organisation, including the degree of satisfaction, trust and support which exists' (p. 45).

5 Development strategies: 'the mechanisms and methods for managing and changing the school, the decision-making strategies, the reward and incentive structure, leadership styles

and procedures for keeping values, relations and structures in balance' (p. 46).

Although it is important to separate out these dimensions, an important point to recognise is the dynamic interdependence between them. Even though teachers may appear to be relatively autonomous in their own classrooms, their behaviours, attitudes and feelings about their work are influenced by the organisation within which they work, and this may become very evident when a proposal for even limited curriculum change is attempted. Each member of the institution, too, has a unique perspective on the institution reflecting his particular status within it, and his view of the 'reality' of the institution. Schools, too, as institutions are highly political with conflict between different interest groups a normal fact of life, reflecting management's attempt to introduce a new policy or a pressure group's efforts to force management, or colleagues, to recognise their claim to time in the curriculum or some other resource.

Per Dalin's consultants approach the job of working with a school on a systematic basis They negotiate entry and establish a climate of trust and openness, and administer the Guide to Institutional Learning (GIL)' an instrument which provides some of the data on organisational factors. They offer feedback on the emerging picture and engage in dialogue on strengths and weaknesses in the organisation, identify short- and long-term goals, help to formulate a plan for action, and to put the plan into effect. They also maintain links with other schools in the process of change, and evaluate developments. The consultants 'have expertise in the process of educational change . . . they are able to diagnose the school as an organisation, help the individuals and groups in the school understand the strengths and weaknesses of the school, and institutionalise a process of development'. But their role is not to say what should be done, but rather 'to help the school itself solve its problem' (p. 157).

Underlying Dalin's work is the assumption that schools are *rational,* that is, 'those constituting the decision-making group in a school will try to achieve those goals that are important to them' (p. 176), and 'open' to the study and discussion of practice. But, sadly, the evidence from their studies contradicts this. Most schools 'deal with their day to day problems in a rather piecemeal fashion. Systematic, long range rational planning is not typical of schools'. With regard to openness – 'the adult community within schools too often withdraws to independent classroom activities where they are 'in control'' (p. 177). And yet there are exceptions among both individuals and institutions! Some do have a desire for both rationality and openness, the prerequisites undoubtedly for any serious attempt to improve the quality of performance of teacher and school.

Conclusion

This chapter has focused on evaluation for improvement. It began by discussing children's work as evidence of quality of teaching, and argued that the key to improving practice lay in developing teachers' skills of self-evaluation. But this implied offering teachers adequate support. Headteachers might be able to create an appropriate climate but most lack the requisite professional skills. Consultancy is another means to secure expertise to set the reflective process going. The discussion then moved to the more general question of promoting quality in schools as organisations, and the approach adopted by consultants implementing the IMTEC model. This was based on the assumption that schools are rational and open organisations although the response belied this.

The search for quality implies both rationality and openness. Indeed these are values which should characterise the management of the education system as a whole. They are certainly the basis for any systematic effort to identify, select, certify and promote teachers of quality, the issues which we turn to finally.

7

Appraising Teacher Quality

The education service is labour intensive. In Britain around 600,000 people are employed as teachers, working for LEAs in units (schools) which range from one–teacher establishments to giant comprehensives with over 150 staff. Earlier chapters have stressed the links between the quality of the service schools provide and the quality of the personnel who work within them and lead them. Teachers and headteachers are expected to play a wider range of roles to higher professional standards. Those who manage the education system at national and local level have stressed the importance of recruiting good teachers and retaining them within the education service, but there is a lack of clarity about how to operationalise systems for doing this, and the current administrative structure inhibits development.

Having issued advice to teacher training institutions and LEAs on selecting teachers and appointing headteachers the Government, in England and Wales, has now given itself powers to introduce appraisal schemes for all teachers. But it is inconceivable that improvements in quality will come about unless rational, principled systems of assessment are introduced in which criteria of competence are identified and 'good' evidence is collected in public, open situations on the extent to which candidates and staff display these. Fortunately there are models of such systems available in both public service and commercial organisations in UK and in the education service in USA, and some adaptations for education in this country have been developed. This chapter reviews approaches to appraising quality at the point of selection for initial teacher training, for tenure at the end of the probationary period, and for selection for promotion to the post of headteacher. It also considers routine appraisal, but it argues that the way to introduce appraisal is within the context of formal assessment.

Selection for initial teacher training

Selection for initial teacher training is important because it is the interface between the teaching profession and its future members. It is part of recruitment, and therefore has to be handled with sensitivity and imagination if the education service is to compete with other occupations in attracting candidates with the skills and qualities required, especially at a time when a shrinking number of graduates and highly qualified school leavers are in increasing demand.

Selection systems currently operated by teacher training institutions are notable for the gap between what they claim to be trying to assess and how they actually go about assessing the candidates. Not only is there a lack of match between the skills and qualities and the assessment situation devised – for example, a one-to-one interview to establish liking for children and interpersonal skills – but the handling of candidates is often inconsistent, and sometimes cavalier. Selection is significant for the public standing of the profession, for the base line it provides on candidates' current level of development, and training needs, and for the opportunities it offers for professional partnership (see Wilson, 1986).

The Criteria of Teacher Selection (CATS) project (Wilson and Mitchell, 1987) demonstrated that a principled, feasible, economic selection system could be developed for primary and secondary applicants to teacher training. It identified six criteria for selection:

- oral communication
- written communication
- interpersonal skills
- practical teaching ability
- commitment to teaching
- depth of character (or reflective capacity)

(Two more, viz 'subject vitality' and 'resilience' or the capacity to cope with the stress of handling adolescents, were added when the system was extended in 1987 to selection for secondary candidates in maths and English.) Performance criteria for the initial six were defined in a manual which provided assessors with a guide to the purpose and management of a series of situations which candidates were placed in over a selection day.

These situations included writing tasks, leaderless discussion, a practical teaching task where candidates learned in a group eight words of a code and taught it to another candidate in a one-to-one situation, and a half-hour interview with two assessors, one of whom had observed her in all the morning situations, while the other had read up solely her background information (application form, referee's report, etc.) prior to meeting her.

The system was designed with principles of good personnel assessment in mind. These included:

- The devising of multiple assessment situations likely to provide 'good' evidence relevant to the comprehensive range of criteria.
- The use of multiple assessors (four assessors from college and field saw some aspects of the performance of each candidate) familiar with the skills for teaching being assessed, trained in the principles on which the system operated, and able to exploit the potential for evidence collecting inherent in the situations devised.
- The building in of systematic review at different points in the course of evidence collecting with the intention of suspending final judgments until all relevant data were available.
- Monitoring of the system by a Director of Selection and his assistants to collect evidence on quality of functioning relevant to training for improved quality of implementation.
- Systematic treatment of candidates in terms of providing prior information as to the purposes of the selection day and the situations they would encounter, and the uniform treatment of candidates in these different situations.

These principles have universal acceptance in personnel assessment terms: a system which meets these criteria will be a valid means of assessing candidates and produce reliable evidence for rank ordering on suitability for training. But the quality of a system also has to be judged in such practical terms as customer and client satisfaction, value for money, flexibility and capacity for development. The evidence from four years of operating the system suggests that the following criteria are met too:

- Feedback collected both formally and informally indicates that candidates view it as challenging and relevant for deciding on who should be admitted to teacher training. Candidates 'on course' appear to exhibit more flexible attitudes, perhaps a reflection of the challenge they faced in securing entry.
- The selection system is operated by lecturing staff from college, and teachers from primary and secondary schools in the college's vicinity. It is administered by an external director, and visitors from organisations with an interest in teacher selection can attend. (Visitors have included senior management from other teacher training institutions, HMI, education authority administrators, careers advisory services, etc.) With very few exceptions there has been an enthusiastic endorsement of the design of the system: a particularly impressive feature is the way in which field assessors have volunteered each year to devote time to orientation (half day) and serving (three or four days per year).
- Value for money is something of concern to all Scots! But the time costs of the selection system have to be set against the costs of conventional systems (which give poor quality data on candidates) and the spin-offs in terms of customer and client satisfaction, and the partnership between college and field staff which has been fostered through working together in a situation of equals. Another way of viewing costs is as investment.
- Flexibility and capacity for development has been demonstrated through the extension of the system to cater for secondary candidates, and the recognition that within the basic model it is possible to introduce further activities which will reflect growing awareness of the most predictive kinds of evidence to collect on candidates.

The significance of this selection system is that it is a viable model, which could be exported to other institutions which wished to improve the face validity, that is, the plausibility of their selection system. (Predictive validity, is a different and altogether more complex issue, although there is evidence that selection systems with good face validity also have high predictive validity.) A common process could be implemented locally thus giving an institution the dual benefits of a principled set of procedures operated by local field and college staff on its own campus. But current administrative arrangements mean there is little pressure on institutions to justify their selection systems.

Selection for headship

The programme described above was devised in response to an invitation from the host college to advise on the selection of applicants for a new four-year BEd (CNAA) degree. The POST project (Morgan *et al.*, 1983) investigated current practice in the selection of secondary headteachers in England and Wales, and also studied how other agencies such as the Civil Service, the National Health Service, and industrial and commercial organisations selected. Its recommendations for improvement were supplemented in a handbook (Morgan *et al.*, 1984) which provided a job description of the secondary school headteacher and the knowledge/skills required to undertake the job competently, together with exemplar materials and an extensive summarising case study of the process of selecting a head. More recently the research team has reported a survey of headteachers at work (Hall *et al.*, 1986) to which reference was made in Chapter 3.

The job of the head can be divided into four 'tasks' and related sub tasks. Some examples are provided below:

Educational: identifying school goals, determining the academic/pastoral curriculum, establishing school ethos, deploying resources
Management – leadership and human relations: determining school policy-making procedures, deploying staff, evaluating standards and record-keeping, and maintaining the fabric of the building
Management – conceptual and operational: motivating staff and pupils, developing staff, resolving conflicts, and communicating.
External accountability and community relations: in relation to governors and LEA, parents and the general community, employers and external groups.

The following competencies required to do these tasks were also listed: knowledge of educational policy, management knowledge, problem analysis, judgment, organisational ability, decisiveness, leadership, sensitivity, oral communication, written communication.

By drawing up a matrix of each task in relation to the competencies, it becomes possible to evaluate their relative importance for selection decisions. The extent to which candidates possess these different skills can be assessed by putting them in a range of situations on which public evidence on their competence can be obtained. On the basis of this evidence, suitably trained assessors can make judgments of the overall quality of different candidates.

While a number of LEAs in Britain have shown interest in developing some aspects of the documentation and procedures required for implementing such a scheme, it is in USA that the National Association of Secondary School Principals (NASSP) has established such a system. NASSP selection programmes extend over two days of intensive work in which candidates are given typical tasks a school principal faces, including writing memos and letters to parents, interviewing and resolving serious school problems and issues. Participants are observed by highly trained assessors who assess them on twelve dimensions of behaviour: problem analysis, judgment, organisational ability, decisiveness, leadership, sensitivity, stress tolerance, oral communication, written communication, range of interest, personal motivation and educational values. Successful candidates then enter an accreditated pool from which the Boards affiliated to NASSP appoint. Unsuccessful candidates may present themselves for reassessment after a suitable interval in which they have been offered in-service opportunities to develop the skills on which they were perceived to be deficient.

Development of a 'post' system of selection of senior staff in schools in Britain is obviously hampered by the current LEA structure and the unwillingness of any agency representative of employers or of teachers to invest in this field. Yet is hard to see how improvements in the quality of selection for promotion can come about until some such system is established. When headship is so universally agreed to be the crucial factor in the quality of a school, it is difficult to explain the lack of action on this issue.

Formal assessment of teachers at other stages of the teacher's career

Selection for initial teacher training and selection for promotion are points in the teacher's career at which some kind of formal assessment of suitability is invariably required by those who are going to have to live with the decision. There are two other points: selection for appointment to first (and subsequent) teaching post, and assessment for tenure on the completion of probation. Neither of these assessments is currently made with any rigour, or even with any clearly defined criteria in mind.

In appointing staff to ordinary teaching jobs LEAs have to balance the claims of 'returners' (ex-teachers who are now eligible for a teaching post) with college leavers. Although LEAs claim (like the teacher training institutions) to want to appoint the 'best' candidates, their methods of screening are as undeveloped as those operated by most colleges. Consequently an opportunity to collect good data on applicants from a personnel management point of view is lost, and highly regarded college leavers may be puzzled at their failure to secure a teaching post, and be 'lost' to the system. While LEAs may face logistical problems in handling the number of applicants in a time of teacher surplus, administrative solutions could be devised if there were greater central direction to the management of the teaching force.

However, the granting of tenure on the successful completion of probation is an even more crucial concern. Recommendations for tenure are based on the reports of advisers to the DES in England and Wales, and of headteachers to the General Teaching Council in Scotland. Reports are based on impressionistic evidence on a restricted range of aspects of performance. In some cases a recommendation to grant tenure is made without the probationer having been observed in the classroom. In consequence, these assessments prove unhelpful for ridding the profession of all but its most inadequate members and, more seriously, fail to exploit the possibility of providing evidence on how teachers' professional competence actually develops in the first two years of a career in teaching.

Edwin Bridges' study (1985) of incompetent teachers in California found that incompetence appeared to mean persistent failure in one or more of the following respects:

- failure to maintain discipline;
- failure to treat students properly;
- failure to impart subject matter effectively;
- failure to accept teaching advice from superiors;
- failure to demonstrate mastery of the subject matter being taught;
- failure to produce the intended or desired results in the classroom.

Bridges points out that there are many pressures on administrators to tolerate and protect the poor performer, but these are balanced by the need to be responsive to parental complaints, by declining enrolments (and the need to shed teachers), and by accountability arguments. 'Salvage' attempts to help incompetents improve are invariably unsuccessful.

Bridges argues for a stringent test of competence being developed before tenure is granted: 'I'm inclined to make it as hard for teachers to obtain tenure as it is for them to lose tenure' (p. 131). He argues for an evaluation system with the following features:

- Defensible criteria, i.e. criteria of knowledge of subject matter, ability to impart the knowledge effectively, ability to maintain classroom discipline, ability to maintain suitable classroom climate, ability to establish rapport with parents and students, and 'flair', i.e. ability to contribute something of special value or significance to some or all students (such as special talents in art or music), but these defined more precisely so that teachers and evaluators know the performance expectations in respect of each.
- Multiple sources of evidence, for example, observations of headteachers, pupil performance, teacher-made materials, teacher comments on pupils' work, peer observations, student ratings, parent views, and self-evaluations.
- Multiple assessors, viz, a Tenure Committee of three who bring different perspectives (administrator, colleague, and experienced outsider) to bear on the available evidence.

Such an assessment scheme could collect comprehensive evidence on teacher development in planning, delivering and evaluating the curriculum thus providing the basis for imaginative staff management. Of course, one of the wider implications of such a system would be the provision of adequate support and guidance to probationers. Teachers who did not demonstrate the development necessary to secure tenure might be offered an additional short-term contract, or would have the contract terminated.

Teacher appraisal

In the light of the above it is paradoxical that teacher appraisal is the aspect of teacher assessment which is currently receiving most attention, at least in England and Wales. Appraisal is highly contentious, partly because DES has emphasised its role in management (implicitly linking it to merit pay in the 1987 imposed salary settlement), and partly because it is an issue in the dispute between teachers and their LEA employers. The DES objective of establishing a national scheme from September 1988 – which involved funding a project whereby six LEAs combined in a consortium to develop pilot schemes for teacher appraisal – was based on an agreement drawn up in June 1986 in an ACAS (Advisory, Conciliation and Arbitration Service) working panel.

According to Agnes McMahon (1987) the project intended to develop a tested set of procedures and documents for all teachers, including headteachers, to ensure that appraisal was appropriately conducted, and the data so derived recorded and acted on in a proper manner. These procedures and documents could then be adopted by non-participating LEAs.

ACAS's definition of appraisal is that is is '. . . not a series of perfunctory periodic events, but (as) a continuous and systematic process intended to help individual teachers with their professional development and career planning, and to help ensure that the in-service training and deployment of teachers matches the complementary needs of individual teachers and the schools'. It relates to induction of probationers, access to in-service training, career management, guidance, counselling and training for teachers experiencing performance difficulty, and reference writing in connection with staff appointments.

Appraisal raises five interrelated questions:

1 How is appraisal to be made acceptable to the teaching profession?

2 What evidence on teacher performance is to be collected?
3 Who is to collect the evidence?
4 How is the evidence to be used?
5 What resources are to be made available for introducing and maintaining appraisal systems and meeting the needs thereby identified?

Making appraisal acceptable to teachers

In some ways winning acceptance of appraisal is the most difficult problem. The dispute over contract, conditions of service and salary makes teachers view appraisal with suspicion. This is certainly one reason why those headteachers who have already introduced appraisal schemes have put an emphasis on the staff development benefits it can bring. But it does seem odd for government to set so much store on this new, and relatively untried, form of teacher assessment, when assessment at other points in the process of entry to, and progress within, a career in teaching is so badly handled. If appraisal were to be linked initially to the assessment of probationers, it would be serving a purpose that the majority of teachers would willingly support.

The second factor which will influence teachers' attitudes is the principles on which it is based. It has been proposed (see Nisbet, 1986) that schemes should be beneficial, fair, comprehensive, valid, open, practicable and effective in producing change. The following sections indicate how these criteria might be operationalised.

The evidence to be collected

Many of the appraisal schemes currently in use amount to little more than an interview with a member of the school management team to review 'needs'. ACAS says that classroom observation 'will be a central feature of appraisal', but how performance is to be judged is still being investigated. This book has argued that teacher quality in the classroom is a reflection of work in planning and resourcing teaching, as well as in the management of face-to-face encounters with pupils. Evidence on all these aspects must be collected if a rounded view of quality is to be taken. This could mean that teachers should compile folios of the resources they have developed for teaching and assessing, and indicate how their class programmes reflect school and LEA policy statements.

With regard to classroom performance the emphasis must be on *describing* teacher performance rather than judging it. Key considerations include having the teacher outline *in advance of teaching* the purpose the lesson is designed to serve, the reasons why these purposes are important, and the means by which they will be realised. As the teacher is observed putting her plan into effect, a record is maintained of what she does and says. The facts of the lesson are recreated subsequently when the discussion centres on the relationship between plan, implementation and perceived effectiveness in terms of what the pupils were required to do and the success they enjoyed in doing it. Subsequently the discussion may explore the worthwhileness of the lesson plan itself, and the extent to which it reflects school policy, the variety and challenge posed to the learner in the way the plan was conceived, and the professional skill deployed in exploiting the potential of the lesson and managing learners in a manner which maximised 'on task' behaviour. Such discussion must occur immediately after the teaching episode if recollections and perceptions are to be fresh enough for helpful discussion to take place.

From this interview and observational evidence, judgments could be made about the quality of different aspects of planning, the relationship between planning and implementation, the skill in realising plans of different inherent strengths and weaknesses, and the teacher's capacity to reflect on and self-evaluate her own performance. Handled with tact such an approach could assist teachers to pinpoint strengths and weaknesses constructively.

Who is to collect the evidence?

Multiple assessors are required for appraisal as for other forms of teacher assessment. They should be drawn from different constituencies so that the person being appraised is viewed from a number of different perspectives. An ideal arrangement would be a team of three persons – one from the subject's own school, one from a neighbouring school, and one from the advisory service or a training institution. While some of the evidence collecting tasks may be delegated to a single member of the team, the observational aspects would need to be viewed by all. Assessors would need to be trained and selected on the basis of training performance so that appraisal operated in a standard way for all. The more staff who are involved as assessors, and understand what appraisal is for, the higher the level of cooperation that may be anticipated.

How is the evidence to be used?

Unless the evidence collected in the process of appraisal is valid, the use to which it is put could further damage morale amongst teachers. Invalid evidence is not worth collecting, but valid evidence, if it is to be used *beneficially* – as all who argue for appraisal claim – must be linked to a development programme which will provide support for staff. Undoubtedly an appraisal system will put pressure on the weakest staff, some of whom will resign. One issue which will surface is the balance to be struck between diverting resources to aid the least competent, who persist in the profession, compared to the most able who wish to extend their range of skills. Bridges' evidence is that weak teachers do not improve, and, if this is the case, it argues for greater investment in assessment at the points of entry to a career in teaching.

What resources are to be made available for appraisal?

A principled, developed appraisal scheme will cost time and money. The time costs arise from the need to train appraisers, and to conduct appraisal, since time lost to conventional teaching will be considerable. Extra staff may need to be recruited, and funds earmarked to enhance the structure of opportunities for staff development. The system will need to be monitored so that its effectiveness can be gauged, 'effectiveness' being judged in terms of benefit both to the individual and to the functioning of the school as an institution.

Conclusion and implications

The quality of the education service depends ultimately on the quality of the people who staff it. In this chapter the emphasis has been on assessing and developing people for key roles in teaching and management. Let us now integrate the themes addressed in earlier chapters in Figure 7.1 to create an overall picture.

In Chapter 2 it was argued that personal capacity (i.e. the skill the teacher brings to the different aspects of her role) and match (i.e. having the appropriate personal and contextual resources for the job in hand) are the two key ideas for improving the quality of schools.

Line 1 of Figure 7.1 identifies the steps involved in identifying and developing personal capacity in (A) teachers and (B) managers of schools. The research reviewed indicates how this could be done – but if improvements in personal capacity and match are to occur, the overall management of the education service also needs to be addressed.

The central part of the Figure indicates that schools exist in specific contexts. Their clients and customers have varied and

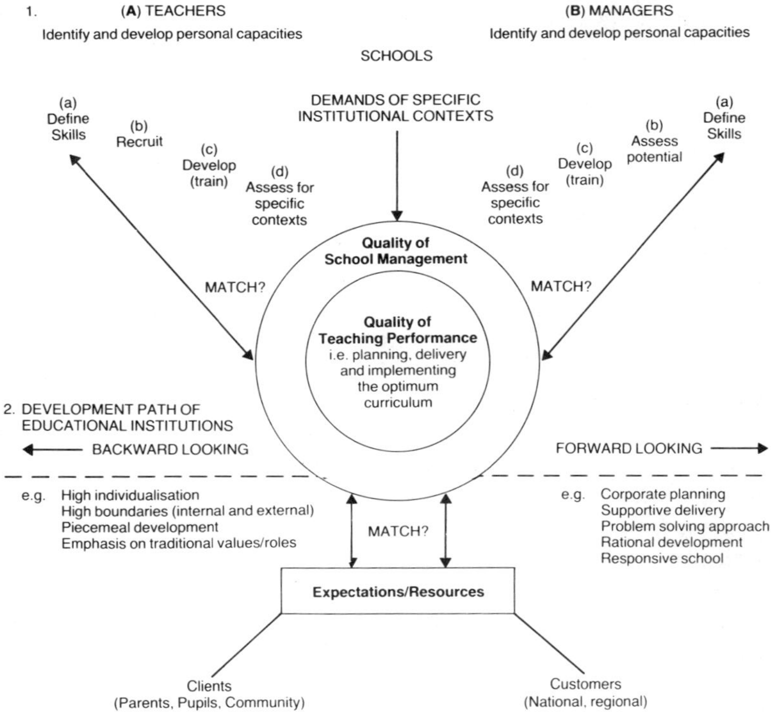

Figure 7.1. Developing Personal Qualities and Match for Improving Teacher Quality in Schools

developing expectations and also provide them with resources for functioning. At the heart of a good school is quality teaching performance. The quality of the individual teacher's work of planning, delivering and evaluating the optimum curriculum for the individual learner is heavily influenced by the quality of school management.

Within the job situation, individual functioning depends on the quality of the match between the different factors involved. Thus successful school management depends on appointing a highly trained manager with the right background and approach for the community in which his school happens to be located. Good teaching depends on the ways in which school management deploy and support staff; and, unless resources are adequate, expectations will be only partially realised.

Line 2 indicates the development path of educational institutions. Institutions may be characterised as 'backward looking' or 'forward looking' in terms of the changing perspectives reviewed in the first chapter. Forward-looking institutions are characterised by a creative corporate management which is sensitive and responsive to new expectations of clients and customers.

The wider question, however, is the management of the public education service as a whole. The days of the current structure are undoubtedly numbered. The ongoing experiment in delegation of financial responsibility in Cambridgeshire (Burgess, 1987) indicates that LEA schools can be managed more effectively when they operate independently: 'All the heads have . . . become better educational managers because of their management of finance' (p.186).

In terms of staff management, an independent national agency is required. Some of the most successful commercial multinationals present a model of efficient caring management in which staff are viewed as an investment and the key resource for their institution's capacity to respond effectively to change. An agency modelling best practice in such institutions would have responsibility for managing the teaching force – in recruiting, selecting, training and deploying teachers. Recruitment would be based on an attractive national career structure and reward system. Selection for initial training would be to the education system rather than to the training institution and it would be undertaken in a principled, standard way. Teacher training would deliver on performance criteria. The agency would devise and monitor effective systems of appraisal for tenure, and create extended interview procedures to identify headteachers of the future. Career management would be at a national level, ensuring that teachers with higher potential experienced a variety of demanding and challenging roles within the education service.

The agency would also exercise important management functions in relation to schools, in time replacing LEAs. It would require schools to articulate the skills and competencies they will develop in pupils across all aspects of the curriculum and indicate the criteria they expect to meet. Quality control would be exercised through a system of accreditation, while national examinations would continue to provide evidence on standards, subject to control of relevant variables (Gray and Jesson, 1987). The agency would also fund research into competency models of curriculum.

Improving quality in education means BIG CHANGE. It means change in management, in the ways staff are hired, trained and nurtured, in marketing the curriculum to meet client and customer needs, and in the evaluation of schools. Big change is easier to bring about than little change if those most affected perceive it to mean a desired improvement. It is time for a paradigm shift in our conception of how the education system should be managed. The changing perspectives with which this book began reflect piecemeal adaptation within old frameworks; the current twin demands of accountability and quality imply perspective changes through revolutionising the structures within which schools operate, defining criteria of competence, and offering attractive, varied and challenging careers to those, at whatever level in the system, with the capacity to promote effective learning.

Bibliography

Advisory, Conciliation and Arbritration Service (ACAS)(1986) *Teachers' Dispute ACAS Independent Panel:* Report of the Appraisal/Training Working Group, mimeo.

Austin, G.R. and Gerber, H. (eds) (1985) *Research on Exemplary Schools.* London: Academic Press.

Barnes, D. (1982) *Practical Curriculum Study.* London: Routledge and Kegan Paul.

Bennett, N., Desforges, C., Cockburn, A. and Wilkinson, B. (1984) *The Quality of Pupil Learning Experiences.* London: Lawrence Erlbaum Associates.

Berliner, D.C. (1985) 'Effective classroom teaching: the necessary but not sufficient condition for developing exemplary schools' in **Austin, G.R. and Gerber, H.** (eds) *Research on Exemplary Schools.* London: Academic Press.

Black, H. and Dockrell, B. (1980) *Diagnostic assessment in secondary schools : a teachers's handbook.* Edinburgh: Scottish Council for Research in Education.

Bloom, B.S. (1978) *Human Characteristics and School Learning.* Maidenhead: McGraw Hill.

Boud, D. and McDonald, R. (1981) *Educational Development through Consultancy.* Guildford: Society for Research into Higher Education.

Bridges, E. (1985) *The Incompetent Teacher.* Lewes: The Falmer Press.

Bruner, J.S. (1965) *Man: A Course of Study (MACOS).* Cambridge (USA): Education Development Center Inc.

Burgess, T. (1987) 'Decentralised budgeting in Cambridgeshire' in **Harrison, A. and Gretton, J.** (eds) *Education and Training UK 1987.* Newbury: Policy Journals.

Cameron-Jones, M. (1985) *Focus on Teaching: Project Report.* Edinburgh: Moray House College of Education, mimeo.

Connelly, F.M., Dukacz, A.S. and Quinlan, F. (eds) (1980) *Curriculum Planning for the Classroom.* Toronto: Ontario Institute for Studies in Education.

Dalin, P. and Rust, V. (1983) *Can Schools Learn?* Windsor: NFER/Nelson.

Davies, W.J.K. (1978) *Implementing Individualised Learning.* London: Council for Educational Technology.

De Luca, C. and Black, H. (1979) 'Collaborative research from both sides of the same fence' in *Scottish Educational Review* **11** (2) 125-32.

Department of Education and Science (1975) *A Language for Life* (Bullock Report). London: HMSO.

Department of Education and Science (1977) *Ten Good Schools.* London HMSO.

Department of Education and Science (1978) *Survey of Primary Education in England and Wales*. London: HMSO.

Department of Education and Science (1981) *The School Curriculum*. London: HMSO.

Department of Education and Science (1983) *Teaching Quality*. London: HMSO.

Department of Education and Science (1985) *Better Schools*. London: HMSO.

Entwistle, Noel (1987) *Understanding Classroom Learning*. London: Hodder and Stoughton.

Fulton, O. (1987) 'The Technical and Vocational Education Initiative: an Assessment' in **Harrison, A. and Gretton J.** (eds) *Education and Training UK*. Newbury: Policy Journals.

Gibbs, G. (1981) *Teaching Students to Learn – A Student Centred Approach*. Milton Keynes: Open University Press.

Gow, L. and McPherson, A. (1980) *Tell Them From Me*. Edinburgh: Aberdeen University Press.

Graham, D. (1985) *Those Having Torches...Teacher Appraisal: A Study*. Ipswich: Suffolk Education Department.

Gray, J. and Jesson, D. (1987) 'Exam results and local authority league tables' in **Harrison, A. and Gretton, J.** (eds) *Education and Training UK 1987*. Newbury: Policy Journals.

Hall, V., Mackay, H. and Morgan, C. (1986) *Headteachers at Work*. Milton Keynes: Open University Press.

Hargreaves, D., Hestor, S.K. and Mellor, F.J. (1975) *Deviance in Classrooms*. London: Routledge and Kegan Paul.

Hawes, H. and Holderness, W. (1984) *Children's Work as an Indicator of Quality*. London: Department of International and Comparative Education, University of London Institute of Education.

Hirst, P. (1974) *Knowledge and the Curriculum*. London: Routledge and Kegan Paul.

Holt, M. (1983) *Curriculum Workshop*. London: Routledge and Kegan Paul.

Hughes, J.M. (ed.) (1984) *The Best Years?* Edinburgh: Aberdeen University Press.

Kerry, T. (1984) 'Analysing the cognitive demands made by classroom tasks in mixed ability classes' in **Wragg, E.C.** (ed.) *Classroom Teaching Skills*. Beckenham: Croom Helm.

Kirk, G. (1986) *The Core Curriculum*. London: Hodder and Stoughton.

Laslett, R. and Smith, C. (1984) *Effective Classroom Management*. Beckenham: Croom Helm.

Law, W. (1984) *Uses and Abuses of Profiling*. London: Harper and Row.

Lawton, D. (ed.) (1986) *School Curriculum Planning*. London: Hodder and Stoughton.

McMahon, A. (1984) 'Reviewing and Developing the Curriculum: the GRIDS Project' in **Skilbeck, M.** (ed.) *Readings in School-Based Curriculum Development*. London: Harper and Row.

McMahon, A. (1987) *Teacher appraisal schemes in England and Wales*, mimeo.

Miller, K. (ed.) (1970) *Memoirs of a Modern Scotland*. London: Faber.

Morgan, C., Hall, V. and Mackay, H. (1983) *The Selection of Secondary School Headteachers*. Milton Keynes: Open University Press.

Morgan, C., Hall, V. and Mackay, H. (1984) *A Handbook on Selecting Senior Staff for Schools*. Milton Keynes: Open University Press.

Moskowitz, G. (1978) 'The classroom interaction of outstanding foreign language teachers' in *Foreign Language Annals*.

Nisbet, John, D. (1986) 'Appraisal for improvement'in **Stones, E. and Wilcox, B.** (eds) *Appraising Appraisal.* Birmingham: British Educational Research Association.

Nixon, J. (ed.) (1981) *A Teacher's Guide to Action Research.* London: Grant McIntyre.

Open University (1981) *Curriculum in Action.* Milton Keynes: Open University Press.

Pearce, J. (1986) *Standards and the LEA.* Windsor: NFER/Nelson.

Peel, E.A. (1960) *The Pupil's Thinking.* London: Oldbourne.

Peters, T. and Austin, N. (1984) *A Passion for Excellence.* Glasgow: Fontana.

Pirsig, R.M. (1976) *Zen and the Art of Motor Cycle Maintenance* London: Corgi Books.

Rogers, R. (1987) 'Special Education: Parents, Education Authorities and the 1981 Act' in **Harrison, A. and Gretton, J.** (eds) *Education and Training UK 1987.* Policy Journals.

Romiszowski, A. (1981) *Designing Instructional Systems.* London: Kogan Page.

Romiszowski, A. (1984) *Producing Instructional Systems.* London: Kogan Page.

Rowntree, D. (1982) *Educational Technology in Curriculum Development.* London: Harper and Row.

Salzberger-Wittenberg, I., Henry, G. and Osborne E. (1983) *The Emotional Experience of Learning and Teaching.* London: Routledge and Kegan Paul.

Schon, D. (1983) *The Reflective Practitioner.* London: Temple Smith.

Scottish Education Departmemt (1986) *Proposals for Simplification,* mimeo.

Selmes, I. (1986) *Improving Study Skills.* London: Hodder and Stoughton.

Shayer, M. and Adey, P. (1981) *Towards a Science of Science Teaching.* London: Heinemann.

Simpson, M. and Arnold, B. (1983) 'Diagnostic tests and criterion referenced assessments : their contribution to the resolution of pupil learning difficulties' in *Programmed Learning and Educational Technology,* **20** (1) 35–45.

Skilbeck, M. (ed.) (1984) *Readings in School-Based Curriculum Development.* London: Harper and Row.

Spencer, L. (1983) *Soft Skill Competencies.* Edinburgh: Scottish Council for Research in Education.

Tamir, P. (1986) 'Teachers' autonomy in a centrally developed and controlled curriculum : an Israeli view' in *Scottish Educational Review,* **18** (2) 86–92.

Taylor, P.H. (1967) *How Teachers Plan Their Courses.* Slough: NFER.

Thornton, G. (1986) *APU Language Testing 1979–83.* London: Department of Education and Science.

Travers, R.M.W. (1981) 'Criteria of good teaching' in **Millman, J.** (ed.) *Handbook of Teacher Evaluation.* New York: Russell Sage Foundation.

Waterhouse, P. (1983) *Managing the Learning Process.* London: McGraw Hill.

Wilson, J.D. (1981) *Student Learning in Higher Education.* Beckenham: Croom Helm.

Wilson, J.D. (1986)' Ten reasons for investing in developed selection procedures' in *Journal of Further and Higher Education,* **10** (3) 57–66.

Wilson, J.D. (1987) 'Sixteen Plus Exams: Lessons from Scotland in **Harrison, A. and Gretton, J.** (eds) *Education and Training UK 1987.* Newbury: Policy Journals.

Wilson, J.D. and Mitchell, L. (1985) 'Developing a policy for selecting primary teachers' in *Journal of Education for Teaching,* **11** (3) 264–79.

Index